RELIGIOUS INQUIRY

RELIGIOUS INQUIRY

An Introduction to the Why and How

In science, I missed the factor of meaning;
and in religion, that of empiricism.

C. G. Jung

SAMUEL SOUTHARD

Abingdon   Nashville

RELIGIOUS INQUIRY: AN INTRODUCTION TO THE WHY AND HOW

Library of Congress Cataloging in Publication Data

Southard, Samuel.
  Religious inquiry: an introduction to the why and how. Bibliography:
p. 117. Includes index. 1. Theology, Practical—Research. I. Title.
BV4.S68   230'.07'2   76-20449

ISBN 0-687-36090-0

MANUFACTURED BY THE PARTHENON PRESS AT
NASHVILLE, TENNESSEE, UNITED STATES OF AMERICA

Acknowledgments

This book began as an invitation from James L. Travis and Douglas C. Turley for lectures on research to the Association of Mental Hospital Chaplains. It was strengthened by a later invitation from Kempton Haynes to prepare an "Introduction to Research" for the Southeast region of the Association on Clinical Pastoral Education. Other chaplains who read the manuscript or provided helpful comments on research questions were: Harold Yoder, Jack Gleason, Raymond Carey, John Tisdale, Richard Dayringer, William J. Johnson.

The original subject matter was broadened for use in the field studies of doctor of ministry programs. The manuscript was strengthened by the suggestions and reviews of Harold Songer, Newton Fowler, Donald Beisswenger, Liston Mills, Clyde Steckel, and James Dittes.

Since I have no specialized training in research I was anxious to obtain the viewpoints of professionals in the field, which were provided by Douglas Johnson, Martin Bradley, William A. Koppe, John Niles Bartholomew, and David Moberg.

Beyond specialized uses of *Religious Inquiry* by chaplain interns or students in a doctor of ministry program, the book is written for use by pastors or denominational officials who want to collect and evaluate evidence at the grass roots level. James C. Massey was especially helpful in this area.

Contents

1. Research Is Your Business

Religious inquiry is the orderly observation and interpretation of attitudes and behaviors that relate to the transcendent element in men or movements. I use the broad term "inquiry" to avoid the narrow picture of "research." The latter term has often been bound by the intense vision of graduate assistants in white coats among bubbling retorts and test tubes. Or we think that research is only "experimental," and that conjures up visions of dogs salivating to the sound of bells or pigeons who push a button for corn to drop into their cage. That kind of study seems far away from religion and beyond the training of clergy.

But long before Pavlov demonstrated stimulus-response behavior under controlled laboratory conditions, American ministers were investigating and writing about experimental religion. The very assumptions of religion in the eighteenth and nineteenth centuries were based on demonstration of belief, observation of behavior according to agreed-upon criteria. The bases of research were present in the church long before the term developed a highly technical meaning under the impact of laboratory methodologies.

Today, the demand for religious inquiry has been accentuated by the emphasis upon continuing education, competency-based learning, the doctor of ministry field study requirements, and the insistence that the program of the church be relevant to the needs of the world.

This need can be met when clerics realize that research studies are possible with their training and in their congregations or agencies. But there is a semantic roadblock to this realization, the modern assumptions about the word "experimental." We think today that it designates the exclusive practice of pure scientists. We have forgotten that experimental was formerly associated with the most essential aspects of true religion.

The Religious Meaning of "Experimental"

This is properly Christian experience, wherein the saints have opportunity to see, by actual *experience* and *trial*, whether they have a heart to do the will of God, and to forsake other things for Christ, or no. As that is called experimental philosophy, which brings opinions and notions to the test of fact; so is that properly called experimental religion, which brings religious affections and intentions, to the like test.[1]

With these words, Jonathan Edwards established the original meaning of experimental in the American vocabulary. It was the study of behavior as an index to the heart. Although Edwards admitted that human internal dispositions could not be intuitively seen by others, he argued for the necessity of visible or audible qualifications to others. For the eye of Christian judgment to decide on visible sainthood, it was necessary to scan a person's practice as well as his profession.

In his summary of studies in psychology of religion, James Dittes referred to Edwards' *Religious Affections* as the most notable theological attempt to discern the relationship between the inner spiritual life and the more visible and public.[2] As a principle mover in the Great Awakening of 1740, Edwards was mistrustful of his contemporaries' reliance on dramatic conversion experiences. Out of a firm belief that behavioral and attitudinal evidences of religion could be demonstrated, he evolved twelve objective signs or criteria of holy affection. These distinguished the true workings of God's grace: "Religion consists much in holy affection; but those exercises of affection which are most distinguishing of true religion, are those practical exercises."[3]

The methodology that produced this "profound religious psychology," in the judgment of Perry Miller,[4] was similar to that which might be used by any cleric in his daily practice. In modern research it is labeled "participant observation," since the observer and recorder lives with the situation and is often a participant in the events that he describes. One of the most significant participant observation studies of the twentieth century has been Robert S. and Helen M. Lynd's *Middletown*.[5]

In the late nineteenth century, Charles Booth used participant observation to authenticate *Life and Labour of the People of London* when a sophisticated audience discredited the literary and impressionistic attempts of other reformers to show the poverty and deprivation of the time. In seventeen volumes he poured out a mass of firsthand observations, numerical relationships, and unbiased conclusions. It was an awe-inspiring work not because of the statistics, but because of the realistic descriptions of the actual life of people.[6]

These are examples of what a minister can do with his own training and remain consistent with the purposes of his calling. But the cleric has often been discouraged from research because of a new meaning of experimental that came from the late nineteenth-century studies of Wilhelm Wundt and other physiological psychologists who emphasized controlled laboratory conditions. Their emphasis upon measurable stimulus and response became so extreme that William James referred to this as "brass instrument psychology." By the 1920s, the experimental method had become the basis of behaviorism in the United States. Behaviorism assumed that nothing could be regarded as factual unless it were tested by a known stimulus under controlled conditions to give an observable response. This response was then converted to numbers. Mathematical calculations were performed on these findings, and results reported in objective form.

Various observers began to warn that these studies were as philosophical as they were scientific. They were based upon theoretical positivism which filters all reality through physics. Only that which can be experimentally verified by physical laws is accepted as real.[7]

The trend toward control and measurement became so pronounced that David Bakan, professor of psychology at the University of Chicago, warned that well-designed graduate experiments were moving away from experience toward insignificance. He urged a return to the original meaning of experimental as experience. Early psychologists, like Brentano, had been correct in 1874 when they placed major emphasis upon the word "empirical." An empirical study is careful observation of experience. This is research.[8]

The Need for Empirical Studies

Research is a natural part of religious experience when we get back to the original meanings of experimental and empirical. American religion has been characterized by an emphasis upon concrete accomplishment, either through the individual practice of religion, or cooperation through societies and denominations.[9] We are supposed to demonstrate what we believe. This demonstration calls for empirical studies that are appropriate for clergy in at least four areas.

(1) "What is the relation of inner spirituality to individual conduct and behavior?" This has been a fruitful area of inquiry, from Jonathan Edwards' *Religious Affections* to William James' *Varieties of Religious Experience*. In the last half of the twentieth century, Gordon Allport, Milton Rokeach, Bernard Spilka, and others have developed questionnaires and interview schedules to demonstrate the characteristic thinking of those who have deep, personally felt religious belief and consistent practice versus those who adopt religious attitudes and practices for the sake of social convenience.

During civil rights controversies, a perennial question is, "Why do those who attend church take the most reactionary stands on social issues?" When Campbell and Fukuyama separated the *types* of church participation, they found that three styles of participation reinforced the status quo, but a fourth, the devotional orientation, enabled a worshiper to stand against the prevailing social situation.[10] Research instruments enable us to distinguish varieties of spirituality and demonstrate their relationship to our public practice of religion in life.

(2) "What is the relation of theology and church organization to our changing society?" Answers require systematic inquiry of what people believe, how their belief is related to organizational participation, the degree of open- or closed-mindedness of believers to changes in society, and some indicators of the actual changes that are taking place in society.

Studies like that of Campbell and Fukuyama are moving toward some answers to this complex question. But at the same time, some articulate champions of social change have not availed themselves of the sociological and psychological studies that would demonstrate the precise problems or provide guidelines to solutions. Samuel

Mueller, a sociologist at Loyola University, complained that church members who speak eloquently of "relevance" are using outdated or impressionistic data for their conclusions.

For example, in Harvey Cox's chapter on urban life in *The Secular City*, only three works are cited from sociology. One is the 1887 classic of Ferdinand Toennies, *Gemeinschaft und Gesselschaft*. The second reference is to a 1954 reprint of Toennies. The third is a July 1939 article from the *American Journal of Sociology*, reprinted in 1958.

Professor Mueller asserts that the sources are at least thirty years out of date and were not based on an empirical study. Later research studies cast doubt on their hypothesis that the urban dweller is the social isolate that Cox pictures him to be, based on the early impressionistic studies.[11]

The church will be more relevant to the world when we begin to use the studies that have already been made of the society in which we live.

(3) Changes in the image of the minister have created a demand for some reliable study of what the laity and ministers expect a competent pastor to be. The Association of Theological Schools began such a study in 1974. Volume 1, "Criteria," is available from ATS, P.O. Box 396, Vandalia, Ohio 45377.

Questionnaire studies in the 1960s and 1970s have already indicated that the laity expect the minister to be a spiritual director, a guide to the resolution of moral difficulties. This expectation creates a demand for more empirical observation of the types of problems that ministers are expected to handle: guilt, forgiveness, grief, anger, despair. How are each of these states of being to be identified? How may a minister distinguish the normal and the abnormal, as in cases of real guilt versus scrupulosity? What is the typical course of the feelings, as in the stages of grief? What advice or course of action has been found helpful at various stages of an experience or with particular types of difficulty?

These are questions for the development of a body of knowledge which forms the basis of professional practice. The development of competence in pastoral practice is the crucial test in the early days of a pastorate.[12] As a person matures in ministry, he finds many areas in which additional knowledge and skill are necessary. Among Episcopal priests, the major needs were in social problems, communications, Christian education, public relations, administration, pastoral care, and counseling.[13]

How will the minister meet these needs? One of the learnings from the career development centers for clergy is that a minister must be deliberate and intentional about setting priorities of time, tasks, and themes for pastoral practice.[14] To do this, he will need some study of what he is doing and what the needs are in his congregation. He must be experimental about his own ministry, evaluating his own experiences and assisting others to assess their expression of faith as well.

Assessment of ministry assumes that a cleric does not know everything when he graduates from professional school. We could lay the groundwork for continuing education through the strengthening of field study and the introduction of research studies in every division of the curriculum. As professionals in other fields look at theological education, they are amazed by the assertions that are made apart from empirical verification. After reading Reinhold Niebuhr's *The Self and the Dramas of History*, Carl Rogers wrote:

I am impressed most of all by the awesome certainty with which Dr. Niebuhr *knows*. He knows, with incredible assurance, what is wrong with the thinking of St. Thomas Aquinas, Augustine, Hegel, Freud, Marx, Dewey, and many, many others. He also knows what are the errors of communism, existentialism, psychology, and all the social sciences. His favorite terms for the formulations of others is "absurd," but such other terms as "erroneous," "blind," "naive," "inane," and "inadequate" also are useful. It seems to me that the only individuals who come off well in the book are the Hebrew prophets, Jesus (as seen by Niebuhr), Winston Churchill, and Dr. Niebuhr himself.[15]

Hans Hofmann, a Harvard Theological School professor, replied to Rogers. In his opinion, experimental scientists "should not be tempted to exceed phenomenological results and trespass with their own inadequate conclusions into spheres where the explanation of either ultimate cause or future result is beyond the reach of their experimental means."[16]

Dr. Rogers was puzzled by this comment. It seemed that in the world of Professor Hofmann, "the scientist searches for the truth in the scientific area, and the theologian *has* the truth in the theological area. This must indeed be a comfortable world in which to live, but unfortunately for me, it is not the world I live in."[17]

How can we learn to be competent as ministers without some tested evidence of the problems which our people face, the theory and practice that has proved valuable under varying circumstances, and some awareness of areas that require further investigation? Two hundred years ago, the clergy were the American pioneers in empirical studies, with John Wesley's insistence upon daily diaries and self-inspection, Jonathan Edwards' notes on revivals, and Muhlenberg's verbatim record of his pastoral visits (in *The Journal of Henry Melchior Muhlenberg*).

(4) The Methodist tradition of continual study is now an interdenominational emphasis upon continuing education. The institutionalized form of this, the doctor of ministry degree, requires field study as part of training for "excellence in ministry." When a pastor develops a new program in his church as a field project, evaluation of his efforts is required. But where have ministers learned to evaluate new or existing programs in the church? In a survey of books and periodical literature of the past fifteen years, David Ernsberger of Austin Presbyterian Seminary found only two articles in the journal of the Religious Education Association and two papers by the National Council of Churches on evaluation.[18]

To assist theological faculty and candidates, Marvin J. Taylor has organized evaluator's training workshops and consultations for the Commission on Accrediting of the Association of Theological Schools.[19]

Evaluation, participant observation, peer review, pro—active learning are phrases that recur in conversations about continuing professional education and development of new church programs. The minister needs some knowledge of the theory and practice of empirical investigation in order to be guided toward an effective assessment of his career development.

The purpose of this volume is to provide guidelines and examples for research that will be appropriate in the church and manageable by professionals who have no advanced training in statistics or other quantitative methods. My thesis is that research in religion is a natural and required part of religious experience and life in the church. In the next chapter we will see how scientific observation develops in the everyday life of an alert minister.

2. The Church as a Local Research Center

Research in the church is an opportunity to combine relevance and dependability. Relevance is an answer to the question, "Does this study stir us to action and give us accurate insight on how to proceed?" Dependability states, "The conclusions of this study are required by the methodology and the data."

These desirable characteristics of research are possible in a congregational setting, but the minister is tempted to distort the balance of relevance and dependability. He may seek the security of some standardized means of measurement. But does the standard test measure the phenomenon he wishes to examine? Will it contribute a lifelike answer in a natural setting?[1]

It is more relevant to ask questions that are directly related to the life situation we would explore. This means some sacrifice of the controlled conditions that we often associate with empirical study, but it does increase authenticity and is characteristic of the field studies and program evaluations that will be required of many ministers.

Dependable methods can strengthen the relevance of any study, because credibility is enhanced and more people can rely on the findings. But dependability without relevance is lost motion, even in graduate school.

To emphasize relevance, the first part of this chapter will describe the ways in which empirical findings can come out of everyday professional duties. Once this is accepted, we can turn in the second section of the chapter to the characteristics of research, the procedures that develop dependable results.

Study Where You Are Responsible

Relevant research can grow out of programs for which you are responsible. A key question in the doctor of ministry program at the Southern Baptist Theological Seminary is: "What is your place in the program under investigation?"

When pastors and graduate students begin to use their own resources for research, they may produce positive results. Ed Cliburn was a veteran minister with the common problem of a downtown church—to minister to the neighborhood or move to the suburbs. His doctoral project was an investigation of all city, county, and civic association reports on movement of population and facilities in his town. This was combined with interviews in which officials and citizen decision-makers projected their estimates of population density and number of services available in the next two decades in various sections of the city. When Mr. Cliburn presented his conclusions from analysis of data and interviews to his doctoral committee and to his church, it was obvious that the town was already moving back toward the inner-city. His church would be in a more strategic location in ten years than it had been during the last decade.

The result was not only a revitalization of the downtown congregation, but a new place for the pastor as a lecturer to civic clubs and a consultant on city planning. In a small city with no specific staff for planning, he had gathered essential data and made conclusions that were vitally needed by the entire community.

Research is also relevant when it grows out of specific pastoral concerns. A navy chaplain, Robert Bermudes, observed a distinct pattern of grief reactions in the wives of submarine crewmen who might be away for three to nine months. He tested his observations with a questionnaire that was designed to test his hunches about the stages of grief.

The questionnaire showed the greatest fear to be "being unloved" and "left alone." Chaplain Bermudes then developed friendship and worship groups for the wives which contained an interpretation of the grief process. Several wives expressed immediate relief; their feelings were understood and they did not need to assume that they were going crazy because of depression.

In commenting on this research, Professor Dittes noted that the chaplain was a more confident pastor because of his examination of observations, and he certainly had produced more relevant findings because he wrote his questionnaire on the basis of his own experience with lonely people. Also, he administered his instrument as a pastor, which did not interfere with the reliability of his results.[2]

Both relevance and dependability may be enhanced by a systematic study of observations which are gathered in the daily routine of pastoral ministry. The observations must be comprehensive enough to cover the pertinent questions that would be raised in the research. For example, a routine medical examination requires a physician to ask about all eight systems of the body. A later research study might deal with disturbances of one system but require some examination of records on the other seven systems to rule out any unusual influence of one system upon another. This would be known through an examination of the routine record because it contains information on all functions of the body.

The observations must not only be comprehensive, they

must be systematic. That is, the researcher must have confidence that a study of particular pastoral problems will involve a review of visits to all members of a congregation or a study of all records of persons who sought help from a pastor.

I learned the value of systematic recordings of routine interviews when I was asked as a mental hospital chaplain, "Why are so many patients crazy because of religion?" As I thought back over two years' experience in interviewing, I could not think of many cases in which religion precipitated or seemed to be a gross part of a patient's illness. But the only previous study of the subject in the state had indicated that 17.2 percent of patients had long-term moral and religious conflicts.

As I looked back over the records of interviews with 170 first-admission patients, I found only three patients who talked of any long-term religious conflict. There were four in which religious disturbances seemed to precipitate a psychosis. And there were twenty-three in which religion was part of the language or ideation of the patient for a few weeks of acute disturbance. In 50 percent of the patients' records I found no religious ideation or interest, even though I had asked each one about these issues in one or more visits.

The difference between the 1.8 percent long-term conflict in my experience and the 17.2 percent in the previous study was the way in which information was gathered. My records came from routine visitation of all first-admission patients. The previous study was made by graduate students who went to many wards of a state hospital to talk to any patients who might be attracted to a chaplain. As we would expect, those who had settled upon religion as the language of their difficulties would often seek out a chaplain. Those with little or no religious interest would remain unseen or silent.[3]

In summary, we can affirm the values of local research when it emerges from a specific pastoral concern, is based on routine, comprehensive records, and/or moves toward an answer to issues for which the researcher has some professional responsibility.

Any professional person can meet in his own practice the basic requirements of scientific investigation:

(1) An intimate familiarity with the subject to be investigated; that is, out of our continuing relationship with people we develop the major questions for research.

(2) A systematic ordering of our observation, through the writing of summaries in which we include the information that is usually helpful from a person in our profession to anyone who would seek assistance. Or the information might be systematic categories of statistics and comments on them under "building construction," "highway density projections," "new zoning regulations," "age of children in new residences," and so forth. Some classification is essential.

(3) An interpretation of our findings that makes sense for our work. If we make the interpretations alone, we must describe why and how we reached conclusions. If others assist us in the interpretation, we should show how much agreement there is between the independent judges.

We are not required to answer all the questions that might be raised from our data; we should develop our data toward classifications that help us to something better in our profession, as the chaplain asked questions about stages of grief that would contribute to better pastoral care.

Unfortunately, the directors of doctor of ministry programs and urban training centers often find clergy to be unsystematic and global in their thinking. We are not selective in our observations; that is, we often do not know what to look for, so we cannot be precise in our conclusions. No one else can be convinced, because we did not identify beforehand what we should see, and were not careful in the way that we looked for answers; for example, drawing conclusions about religion in the psychoses on the basis of random conversations with patients who wanted to speak with a chaplain.

Because of these difficulties in our own professional thinking, we need some of the clarification and rigor that is associated with scientific investigation.

Develop Findings Others Can Follow

The characteristics of research are often described under the label of reliability, scientific, empirical, or experimental. These are labels for the dependability of our study. That is, we should have clearly shown the way that others may follow in knowing what we did and why we came to particular conclusions.

One essential characteristic of a dependable project is the publication of findings in a journal or thesis that is readily available to other persons in the profession.

Since space is limited in professional journals, no more than a summary may be printed there. At least this gives others a chance to know where our material is to be found. For example, the Joint Council for Research in Pastoral Care and Counseling publishes an annual summary of research studies in the field of pastoral care (Virginia Institute of Pastoral Care; 507 North Lombardy Street; Richmond, Virginia 23220).

The problem with a summary is that a report like that of Chaplain Bermudes in the *Journal of Pastoral Care* does not contain references to methodology. What were his questions? How did he decide to interpret the answers? What were the answers? What were the scoring procedures? These questions are usually answered in the original research document which should be available either from the researcher or from a seminary library or professional organization.

Another requirement of dependability is clear definition. Are you describing a subject in such a way that others will be able to identify the same thing? I did not as a graduate student. "At what age were you converted?" was one of the questions I proposed to ask Southern Baptist, Presbyterian, Methodist, and Disciples of Christ theological students. Before I sent out the questionnaire, I submitted it to a panel of judges, one of whom was in an interdenominational divinity school. He politely wrote me, "As an Episcopalian, I was baptized at three months and confirmed by the bishop at age twelve. Please inform me, which age should be recorded as 'conversion'?"

The question of identification should include instructions on the way in which the subject was measured. How is "devoutness" to be defined: (1) by a subject's statement about his inner feeling, or (2) by his answer to a number of questions about devotional life in the church? The latter may include his definition of a Christian as one who prays and reads the Bible daily and attends prayer meetings.[4] The latter approach is more indirect, and more reliable than the former, which may measure anxiety for social acceptance; "yes-sayers" like to look good on questionnaires.

A third requirement of dependability is fortitude. You stand by what you promised to do, even when the results are not to your liking. Once you define a subject for investigation and describe the way in which it will be measured, you are bound to report exactly what you find.

24

An investigator will usually be accurate in a report of the incidence of a behavior or the number of times a certain item was checked on questionnaires. The inaccuracy comes in an interpretation that redefines the subject or the way it was measured. For example, in a study of thirty theological students' choice of the ministry, a researcher found that in the one-hour interview, six students made some mention of sex. Four of the six said that sexual activity before marriage was sinful. The researcher wrote as one of his conclusions that the typical theological student confessed that sex was quite a problem in his youth and had made him feel like a sinner for life.

This study missed another requirement, which is the possibility that another inquirer could repeat the study: identify the subject matter, copy the methodology, use the same type of findings to draw conclusions. We do not know how sex came into the conversation in the interviews, what the students were asked about their feelings on the subject, their sexual practices, or the way in which the interviewer defined sex as a "problem."

The study could have been replicated if the original interviews had been used to collect a pool of subjects that were mentioned by a certain number of students as significant in their decision for the ministry. This would have become a valid base for the development of a focused interview or questionnaire, in which specific subjects were raised for discussion or responses offered for checking. The researcher would commit himself beforehand to a hypothesis such as, "A student who talks about sex as violation of moral standards in terms of adultery or homosexuality will be listed as a person who sees sex as a problem area in his life." We may or may not agree with the statement, but at least we know what he asked and why he drew his conclusion.

A fifth dependability requirement is the systematic building of relationships between findings. Tested description of phenomena leads to tentative explanations, which are tested under varying circumstances to understand the limits or variations of an explanation. After repeated verification of propositions through many trials, some central concept is presented as a unifying explanation. A variety of findings are now capable of classification under some general theory which tells why they belong together.

This has been a difficult expectation of religious studies. Why? For one thing, there never is enough money for empirical studies in religion to be repeated. Only in limited areas can this be attempted, as in the replication of studies on the relationship of social conditioning to church participation. Second, the methodology of graduate studies in theological schools is usually a questionnaire or participant observation. The frequency of answers to a specific question is tabulated by hand to prove or disprove an assumption such as, "Young people who rededicate their lives to religious purposes at a religious retreat will report an earlier age for joining the church than young people who do not make a rededication at the same retreat." The answer may be found without any electronic data processing.

In contrast, most graduate studies in psychology or sociology include the tabulation of scores from several questions to form an index, or indicator of salient attitudes or behavior, and correlatons of one index with another. Usually this is done by instructing a key-punch operator to punch a predetermined space on a three-by-eight-inch card as the answer to a particular question. By electronic sorting, all of the cards that have similar answers to questions 1, 5, 10, and 15 can be accumulated quickly in one pile and counted.

More complicated procedures involve the construction of a matrix in which the relationship of every item in a questionnaire is compared with every other item. This enables the researcher to know the items that are commonly associated in the minds of respondents. Can these items be given a common label, like "personal religious experience" or "personal ties in the congregation"?[5]

The psychological or sociological student expects correlations; his use of electronic data processing makes this possible. Each research study moves toward cumulative results, the development of systematic indexes or classifications.[6]

A sixth requirement of dependability is limited understanding. The empirical investigator does not try to explain more than his data can reasonably justify; he does not try to understand more than others can think through with him when they investigate the same subject for themselves.

In contrast to Bakan's complaint that psychology graduate studies are so methodologically restrictive as to be inconsequential in their conclusions, theological graduate studies may attempt global conclusions on the basis of one tabulation of questionnaire results. For example, a minister concluded one section of his graduate thesis with the assertion that the call to a church vocation was "an almost autonomous experience." This large assertion was based on the majority of affirmative responses he tabulated to one question: "Were you greatly concerned about the approval or disapproval of family or friends?"

A much more limited and realistic understanding of the "call" came in a graduate study which also used questionnaire tabulation, with no complex correlations. The author examined the responses of black and white theological students to questions about family background, religious concepts, and behavior. He concluded that the home was the most important agency for recruitment of ministers, with black ministers reporting less influence than white ministers.[7]

Meaning Without Deception

Relevant research is an orderly inquiry into values that have meaning for us and a group of like-minded people. But, as the examples in this chapter may have shown, we may deceive ourselves in the process of observation, reporting, and evaluation. Or our study may be greeted with skepticism by those who are not of the same mind. Also, people may be searching for some of the same answers that intrigue us, and be frustrated because our inquiry is not organized or presented in a fashion that they can follow.

We can increase the meaning of our investigation for more people if we surround our personal observations with precautions. Then we will be convincing to persons who follow some of the same rules for fact-finding and have an open mind toward the subject that interests us.

The use of scientific methods will decrease deception. Our report will be more reliable. If the study also grows out of a program for which we have responsibility, or is the natural result of routine summaries of our pastoral ministry, we will have both relevance and dependability in one report.

3. The Varieties of Religious Inquiry

In the early twentieth century, many American ministers were so preoccupied with the production of a stereotyped conversion that they missed the rich variety of religious experience that William James sought to describe for them.[1] The same narrowing of methodology and assumptions can occur in religious research, in the preparation of field reports for a doctor of ministry program or in self-study guides for a local church. One student will be sure that he must use a questionnaire, while another searches for a standardized test. Some professors insist on a hypothesis, and others declare that there is no dependable investigation without a control group. Writers in the field are fascinated with one or more requirements for empirical studies. I had to be corrected by the readers of this manuscript against an overemphasis upon replication. As several said, there are many field studies or individual experiences that cannot be exactly duplicated.

So when we come to the question of a type of research for your study, we need to consider a wide range of available styles. The characteristics of dependability, from the previous chapter, should be considered, but only in relation to the appropriateness of any methodology for the subject under study and the amount of responsibility that you, and others, will accept for it.

Some of the methods of research that seem appropriate for religious inquiry are as follows:

(1) In a *review of documents* we analyze the content of church records, biographies and autobiographies, or a set of verbatim interviews to see what they say about a definable subject. We have no control over the original content; we can only approach it for review.

(2) A *sample survey* offers more control of information. We ask a relevant and representative group of people for answers that are significant for a particular inquiry. Usually our interview or questionnaire will tap attitudes, preferences, and opinions along with identifying data such as age, sex, place of residence.

(3) *Field observation* will give us a picture of attitudes and behaviors in their natural setting. The portrayal may be only from the observer's point of view or from his observations plus some of the following ways of gathering data.

(4) One check on the observer's viewpoint is a statement of opinion by the subjects under investigation on some of the questions that need to be answered. In an *area analysis*, the researcher adds his observations to the data that he records from interviews and questionnaires.

(5) When an investigator wishes to concentrate upon specified behaviors or to be sure that he understands the attitudes of individuals on a subject, he will conduct a *focused interview*.

These five types of study are only suggestions. As you look over them, you will see a combination of factors that could be recombined in a methodology most suitable for your own purposes. One factor would be participation of subjects in the investigation, which is maximized in a focused interview and absent in a review of documents. Another element is breadth of information or population, obtained in a sample survey, versus depth of analysis in a focused interview or review of one autobiography. There is also the question of objectivity and subjectivity, which might be combined in field observation. And there are many other issues that could be considered. The reading of research texts, such as I list in the appendix, will stimulate your thinking on other combinations or show you a specific method that seems to fit your questions.

Review of Documents

Documents may range from personal case histories, which Anton Boisen called the "living documents," to biographies, church minutes, denominational statistics. This material is appropriate for several research objectives.

(1) Identifying trends over a period of time,
(2) Demonstrating the validity or invalidity of characterizations of a movement or profession,
(3) Exploration of the key issues or the limitations of some religious question.

From the strictly historical document, biography, or autobiography, we obtain a variety of information which must be analyzed and classified according to the needs of our inquiry. You will lose many needles in the haystack unless you know beforehand the topics and subtopics that are germane to the inquiry. The selection of topics may come from a graduate committee, a panel of interested persons, or a conference of experts that have explored the question. I gained assistance through a conference on motivation for the ministry. The papers for this conference provided the topics that should be investigated in a study of the personal life of a minister. The fifteen topics from these papers provided the headings for five-by-eight-inch cards on which I took notes from the reading of several hundred biographies and autobiographies of Southern ministers. One of these topics was childhood experiences. When Margaretta Bowers raised the question, "Are ministers lonely from childhood?" in *Conflicts of the Clergy,* I found some evidence for a negative answer in a review of the five-by-eight cards on childhood experiences.[2]

A more demanding problem is to review documents under a general topic, such as the class meeting, with no previous study to guide you. Liston Mills undertook this type of historical investigation by establishing a basic thesis from existing historical studies; discipline was related to pastoral care in frontier churches through class meetings that provided watchfulness and supervision. Church minutes and church histories were then checked for evidence of this thesis.[3] The methodological problem was the inaccessibility of the primary documents. Methodist historians told Dr. Mills that the information that he wanted was probably in boxes of unclassified material which were stored in one or more of the libraries in Methodist seminaries. Although some primary documents are inaccessible, I would plead for more use of historical documents in the practical fields of divinity. The historical collections of several denominations are housed in facilities that provide space for researchers, staff who are knowledgeable and cooperative, and primary and secondary sources which are classified by subject.

The "dead" data of church statistics may also prove to be a source of lively interest. Murray Leiffer surprised Methodist officials when he compared manpower trends in a series of General Conference reports. When his report in 1948 demonstrated the steady erosion of active ministers due to death, retirement, and other assignments, a specific campaign was launched to increase candidates for the ministry. This was reflected in a supply of young ministers in 1952 and 1956 that would offset losses through age and disease. Dawson Bryan, an official of the Methodist General Board, said that this dangerous drain on the supply of ministers was almost unnoticed until Dr. Leiffer began to delve into the records.

Of course Dr. Leiffer was using the *reported* gains in membership by Conference to project the manpower needs for clergy in the next four years. Church statistics on membership may be more optimistic than realistic. One enterprising statistician found more Baptists reported as members of churches in one county than the federal census enumerated as total population for the county.[4]

Libraries of taped interviews offer records of live conversations. These are usually studied through some form of content analysis. In *Psychotherapy Research,* edited by Gary Stollak, Gerald Marsden has reviewed a variety of content analysis studies of therapeutic interviews from 1954 to 1964. The data may be transcripts of taped interviews or responses of clients to evaluation questions at the end of each interview. The research calls for specific definitions of characteristics to be studied, the agreement between several raters that excerpts from the interviews have been correctly classified, and some statistical demonstration that one or more characteristics have been consistently identified. Other characteristics may be those of patients (self-awareness, change during treatment, personal acceptance) or characteristics of the therapist (hostility, avoidance, interpretation, support).[5]

In summary, a review of documents does not require consent from individual subjects or the check of their concurrences with the researcher observations. Such review does have the advantage of data that would be accessible to others for replication, whether it be institutional statistics or routine recordings of interviews.

The Sample Survey

One disadvantage of document review is gaps in information that is considered essential for the answering of some research questions. The noted psychoanalytic historian Erik Erickson complained of this as he wrote *Young Man Luther*. As he sought information about Luther and other religious figures, he found that biographers of notable persons wrote under the assumption that the great men had no families. This was an intolerable omission to Dr. Erickson, who had spent his life in a study of the way that character is conditioned by family relationships.

A sample survey remedies some omissions in information by asking a relevant group of people for answers that are considered significant for a particular inquiry. The sample may be representative of all adults in the United States who are not in institutions, as in Gurin and associates' survey *Americans View Their Mental Health*, or it may be confined to people in the churches of one county, members of one denomination, or inmates of one hospital.

The survey denotes some inquiry into broad categories which are appropriate for the sample population, and may go from the dozen questions of a Gallup or Roper poll to the more than five hundred questions asked by Jeffrey Hadden of seven thousand ministers in six denominations.[6]

Since questionnaires are almost universally used in sample surveys,[7] some consent is required from the subject who returns a mailed questionnaire or agrees to an interview. Because the survey is of a general nature, anonymity of the individual is guaranteed. The amount of subject involvement in the research is minimal, since he will not be identified in the final report and usually is not checked on the relationship between answers to the questions and actual behavior.

The survey is more suited for information about attitudes, preferences, and opinions than for the demonstration of behaviors that may be at variance with an ideal.[8]

Ministers could probably reduce the gap between stated opinion and practice by adopting the multidimensional approach to questionnaires that have become standard among social scientists. For example, both attitudes and practices concerning race can be tapped by questions on what people should do in general ("Should blacks have rights to all public services?"), what is right for you (Would you be willing for a black family to move in next door?"), and what has actually happened because of your attitudes ("List the names and addresses of three black persons with whom you have frequent personal or social contact"). When these three dimensions of racial attitudes are compared, we may find a high percentage of affirmative answers on general attitudes, less frequent approval of personal contacts, and little or no evidence of actual relationships.

Despite the gap between written statement and actual practice, which can be minimized through various techniques, there are several advantages to the sample survey. It is an inexpensive method for the collection of general opinions and provides a reasonable amount of objectivity for the analysis of questions concerning people in one locality or institution. Anonymity is usually guaranteed to subjects and the results may be replicated.[9]

Field Observation

The sample survey would probably not be our choice for a study of the transcendent element in religion or its place as a force for man's autonomy. More subjective styles of study would be appropriate for these issues.

Perhaps the most fruitful inquiries in American religion have come through participant observation. This was the methodology of Jonathan Edwards. *The Faithful Narrative* provides a clear and vivid account of the first "great awakening" in the Connecticut valley from the viewpoint of Edwards as preacher, counselor, and observer of religious experiences. This was followed by an investigation of the central question that follows all national revivals, Why do some people grow in the faith while others fall away? *Religious Affections* was a probing of the nature of piety: What are the signs in behavior and attitude that the affections of a convert are "truly gracious"?

The research questions of Edwards' grew out of his pastoral work. *The Faithful Narrative* began in a letter through which Edwards described the revival to a fellow minister and illustrated his observations with the experiences of two persons who were "affected."

The illustrations in *The Faithful Narrative* and *Religious Affections* came from the personal interviews that inquirers requested with Pastor Edwards and from his observations of these people over a period of years in a small Connecticut town where little was hidden from a settled pastor.

In the rush and movement of the modern pastorate, some ministers may wonder at the empirical accomplishments of Jonathan Edwards. But they are similar to the potential of a modern pastorate if the following conditions can be met:

(1) Jonathan Edwards had an inquiring mind that was served by a "transcendent self." That is, he had the ability

to stand apart from what he was doing and view it with critical insight.[10]

(2) Almost everything that Edwards thought or observed was committed to his notebooks. As he considered the signs of religious affections, he had both observations in writing and his own memory as a basis for analysis. The care with which some eighteenth- and nineteenth-century pastors kept records should be an encouragement to ministers in the twentieth century. John Frederick Oberlin, the celebrated social reformer and pastor of the eighteenth century, refused to leave his rural pastorate after twenty years because, among other things, it had taken him that many years to complete the physical, social, and religious histories of all the people in his parish. Now that he really knew his congregation, his pastoral work would be effective. So how could he move at this time?

(3) Edwards could abstract out of his many observations those facts which were pertinent to the questions of his theological system. The mooring of Edwards' thoughts in basic convictions concerning the truth of the gospel and the promise of spiritual gifts were the independent variables with which his inquiries began. A settled conviction concerning some things is a necessary precondition of the freedom with which we may then look at dependent variables. In the case of Edwards, that which could be questioned and analyzed was the way in which people apprehended the truth of the gospel and the signs by which ministers and others could be assured that the spirit had taken hold and was bearing fruit in personal character.

This combination of theological conviction with empirical observation has been characteristic of the great pastor theologians such as Jonathan Edwards, Walter Rauschen-busch, Reinhold Niebuhr, or Harry Emerson Fosdick. Each of these men looked closely at the surroundings in which the gospel was proclaimed and its effects upon individuals. The contribution of their ministry was built upon this combination of spiritual belief and human analysis.

(4) Pastors like Edwards were conversant with scientific theories that were related to the practice of ministries. In particular, Edwards appropriated the psychological theories of John Locke. Starting with Locke, he emphasized the comprehension of abstract ideas. But Edwards went beyond Locke in refashioning the theory of "sensational" rhetoric. He asserted that an idea in the mind is not only a form or perception but also a determination of love and hate. For Edwards an idea was an emotion as well as a concept. The basic theory upon which he built revivalistic preaching was the assertion that ideas and emotions must be combined.[11]

Participant observation continued to be the most common method of religious research in the nineteenth century. But it was eclipsed by the questionnaire in the twentieth century. Anton Boisen returned to the methodology of Edwards, however, in a classification of the personal and social adjustments of church members in his sociological and psychological survey manual, *Problems in Religion and Life* (Nashville: Abingdon, 1946). The recommended classification was followed by a student of Boisen who was pastor of a village church in the Midwest. As reported in *Religion in Crisis and Custom*, the student visited systematically throughout the village and recorded his observations according to the following classifications: faithful, complacent, pagan, mentally ill (difficult, defeated, or distressed), and reorganized. The research question was, "How does religion enter into the common life of our people?" [12] Boisen concluded that the religion of the hamlet was static, since only 4 out of 322 adults had achieved some sort of reorganization in the face of mounting difficulties or threatening defeat.

The Area Analysis

Boisen's student reported his findings in short sentences concerning each person. These were considered to be community judgments of the individual as well as observations of the pastor. From a research viewpoint, the study is limited by the preponderance of subjective evaluations, such as well-balanced, devoted, good-natured, fairly pleasant. These colloquial terms represent the categories by which people judge one another in the community, but they would be difficult to define for someone else in research. How would another pastor know that a person was to be classified as complacent if he and his community raters did not have the same definition of complacent or easygoing as did the student of Boisen and his respondents?

The problem of definition and replication is partially solved by reliance upon objective criteria for the description of a person, such as age, sex, income, education, place of residence. The pioneer in collection of objective data for the churches was H. Paul Douglass. Many of his city-wide surveys were made for church councils in the 1930s and 1940s. The survey reports were a combination of observation concerning sociological characteristics of neighborhoods with a summary of data which is usually available from the city planning council, such as percentage of nonwhite households, median age of housing structures, and so forth. Information on church school attendance and other familiar ecclesiastical information was presented for each district of the city.

Although this type of area analysis was more objective than the participant observation technique of Boisen, it suffers from the major deficiency of uninvolvement of consumers. That is, local congregations and pastors are not specifically involved in planning the survey, designing the questionnaire, interpreting the results. In his later years, Paul Douglass expressed his disappointment at the lack of impact that his surveys had upon local church and council of churches' planning. This pessimism was verified by the field report of John Niles Bartholomew who investigated the impact of a series of professional church and community surveys that had been conducted for twenty-two years by a headquarters staff for the churches of one presbytery. He concluded that "it is apparent from both church records and personal interviews that these surveys made very little impression on the lay leadership of the local congregations." [13]

In the 1950s and 1960s, several denominations moved beyond the general area analysis of a professional surveyor, to the recommendation of a specific set of questions for which answers could be found in church records or in an afternoon canvass of the neighborhood by church members. These self-study guides did produce a factual overview of church and community.

Mr. Bartholomew found the self-study guides to be almost as ineffective as the area survey. Not one of the five churches that participated in self-study could find a copy of the study less than four years later. Also, there was a lack of involvement. Leaders saw the project as a process of data-gathering rather than of planning and implementing new programs to meet changing conditions.

The major limitations of self-studies which are based on attractively printed guides from the denomination have been the static organizational emphasis. The guides are filled with questions designed to measure the "survival goals" of the congregation. Data is collected on budget, attendance, approval or disapproval of program, relationship of sociological characteristics of the membership to sociological characteristics of prospects in the community. As Donald Metz pointed out in his study "Goal Subversion in New Church Development," [14] survival goals are necessary, but should complement "mission goals." Mission goals would be proclamation, nurture, and service to the community.

The emphasis upon mission that came out of the World Council of Churches' Committee on Restructuring of the Congregation has produced a method of field study which involves the congregation. The World Council Committee recommended surveys that would relate knowledge about the congregation to the relevance of the congregation for the actual life of the community. [15] Gerald Jud, a member of the committee, produced a mission-oriented survey guide for his own denomination, the United Churches of Christ. The survey started with the basic assumptions of the congregation concerning its mission in the world and was arranged so that planning and research were part of the same process. [16]

Focused Interviews

The combination of planning and research for mission did not include as heavy an emphasis upon statistical information as the survival-oriented self-study guide. Some statistical information was gathered, but the major emphasis was upon focused interviews. In the United Presbyterian's "Exploration of Mission," church members were trained to interview pastors, members of church committees, community consultants. The major focus of the interviews was upon (1) motivation for survival or mission, (2) procedures to be used in the attainment of goals, (3) results that were expected in terms of direct action and changes of attitudes, and (4) awareness of communication (or the lack of it) between decision-makers in the congregation, and with other congregations. Mr. Bartholomew sought to assess the progress of exploration for mission in the presbytery that had used other types of surveys in the past. He found that church committees had taken the planning function seriously. Several of them had completed the planning phases of their work and had turned over their findings to implementation groups that were formed in the same congregation. It was too early to know if implementation of goals would really follow planning.[17]At least it was clear after one year that the committees had involved a large number of people in the church and in the community in planning for mission.

In general Mr. Bartholomew found the planning-survey-implementation approach to be valuable in (1) its emphasis upon a theological understanding of the mission of the church, and (2) its awareness of the political dimensions of planning.

This emphasis upon theological motivation was confirmed by nine field studies conducted in churches which were in the process of change. The observer, Grace Goodman, found that the initiation for a study of the church in the community and the implementation of findings grew most often out of a study of the Bible and contemporary religious writings, plus a personal search for a meaningful faith on the part of one or more leaders in a congregation. As an unsophisticated layman said to Ms. Goodman in a small country church, "We just sensed our responsibility and when you sense it, there's got to be action." [18]

The observation of Ms. Goodman illustrates the appropriateness of methodology for the question to be considered. Her study was based upon field observations and focused interviews. This allowed her to gain information from a variety of sources about the motivation of persons for their participation in a particular program.

It is difficult to duplicate this type of study without more attention to definitions of terms used in the study, specification of types of persons from whom information will be secured, and control of subjectivity through the rating of conclusions by several independent judges. We obtain through this method a high degree of relevance and responsibility for the study by those who may use it, but dependability is low.

Moving Toward a Balance

The major benefits to local churches have come through studies that have emphasized participation and relevance. Survey research is made a part of planning for program development. Methodology varies with the particular questions to be studied and the amount of money, time, and expertise that is available for research.

But how may relevance and responsibility be balanced with dependability? One solution is to use standardized tests for part or all of the investigations. If the test has been designed for a religious subject and validated with subjects that are usually chosen for a religious sample, then relevance and dependability have been brought close together.

The religious-orientation questionnaire of Gordon W. Allport and J. M. Ross has often been used with questions on some particular variable such as age[19] or mental illness.[20] The usual method is to administer the questionnaire to distinct groups, such as younger and older persons or hospitalized and nonhospitalized persons. Scores of the two groups on the religious orientation scale are then compared.

If a minister wishes to use a standardized test as a part of his research, he would be wise to consult a sociologist, psychologist, or educator who is familiar with tests and measurements. Familiarity means information and experience on the purpose for which a test is designed, what it is to measure, and how it is to be interpreted. It is especially important for a skilled consultant to recommend and perform appropriate statistical analysis of test results, which have usually not been part of the formal training of a minister.

Using a Consultant

Pastors and theological students will be pleasantly surprised at the interest shown by professors and graduate students in psychology, sociology, and related fields in the research design of a religious inquiry. Graduate students are looking for some fresh and relevant area for their dissertations. There are few dissertations in religion because federal research grants were not available for this subject in the first two decades after World War II. Professors are often interested in cooperating on a religious research project for the same reason. Here is an area in which they can make a contribution that will be noticed.

Often there are deeper personal reasons for the cooperation. The subject matter of a religious project may be one that seems significant to a professor or graduate student in a secular field. His theological commitment may not be that of the pastor, but he will consider the subject to be of value in his own philosophy of life or in his professional practice. For example, Phillip Woolcott began a study of religious and nonreligious patients when he was a resident at the Menninger Clinic. It was a question that arose out of his daily work. Dr. Woolcott asked colleagues to name patients who were very religious and patients that were not religious. He found a general inhibition of the subject among psychiatrists. They did not ask about this subject which was of importance to many patients. Dr. Woolcott then began to ask religious and ethical questions of his patients and was gratified to see that they appreciated the concern of at least one psychiatrist about an area of life that was significant to them.

This interest in religion also motivates research and development executives, statisticians, and private research workers to assist ministers in research design, analysis, and interpretation.

What does the consultant expect of the minister in the consultation? (1) A research expert appreciates an opportunity to comment on the original design of a proposal. As we will see in the next chapter, the definition of the problem has much to do with the validity of the results that are obtained. (2) The consultant expects the minister to do the hard work of defining what he wants to study, limiting the area of investigation, and securing the support of subjects for the research. One of the reasons that a consultant will work with a minister is the opportunity to find a sample beyond the usual research group of college sophomores in a required social science class. (3) The consultant will often wish to publish the results of the study as a joint endeavor. It is therefore necessary for the minister to obtain consent from an agency or from individuals who are part of the study to publication in a professional journal. (4) Any financial obligations should be clarified in early conversations. Is a fee to be paid for the consultant's time? Who is to pay for computer time or secretarial service? (5) The analysis and/or conclusions of the consultant should be respected as the minister develops an interpretation of the research. Information from the consultant should be included in the research report and any discrepancy between his conclusion and those of the minister should be noted and explained. (6) The assistance of the consultant should be explained to an agency or church, or to subjects by the minister. A favorable climate should be created by the minister for the beginning of the research. The minister is also responsible for any diplomacy necessary if misunderstandings arise during the research investigation. Finally, the minister is expected to relate any findings of the consultant to the general purposes of his study in a way that seems justified to the agency or research subjects.

But suppose a graduate student is sarcastic in his comments about religion as he meets with a church council to plan the design of a research project? This raises the question of what we should expect of the consultant. (1) The consultant should spend enough time with the minister to ventilate and control any hang-ups that he has about organized religion. This is also an opportunity for the minister to share any preconceptions that he has about research. (2) If the consultation is offered by a university department, the supervising professor is expected to meet with the pastor and graduate students to see that the students are well trained and briefed in the requirements for their participation in the study. This is the time to decide how much the manner and dress of the graduate student will influence the research. (3) The consultant is expected to agree on the step-by-step process in the research to which he will contribute and the dates on which his reports will be due. Fees or expenses are to be paid at the time that each section of the research report is completed. (4) The consultant should translate any statistical analysis into conclusions that can be understood by the laity. This request may be resisted by some experts who believe that a separation is to be maintained between the analysis of data and its interpretation. But in the interest of applied research and the modest statistical training of the average minister, it is a necessity. (5) The consultant should obtain permission from the agency for any use of the research data in the classroom or professional publications. He has a right to his own conclusions concerning the data after he has obtained permission to use it.

If a minister is to be prepared for work with a consultant he will need some information on the definition of his subject and the design of his search. If he cannot obtain a consultant, then he certainly must have some assistance in these areas which are the first step in any type of scientific inquiry. This will be the subject of our next chapter.

4. Defining and Designing the Search

As a young pastor, my idols were Richard Baxter, John Frederick Oberlin, and Anton Boisen. Baxter gave me the challenge of routine calling upon all church members every year. Oberlin strengthened my training to record systematically the information I obtained from those visits. Boisen provided a classification for information that was consistent with the purposes of the church.

After a year of visitation and counseling, I wanted to know how my congregation looked under Boisen's classification. The first step was to note where I saw people and made a record:

> 153 home visits of well members
> 80 home or hospital visits of the sick
> 54 office-counseling sessions
> 46 home visits to prospects.

This told me, and anyone who read my research, that I had seen people in a wide range of circumstances. My population was not confined to a particular segment of the congregation or community, such as troubled people who came to my office for consultation. I felt confident that I was seeing people in healthy as well as in unhealthy states of being. This would be a reliable group from which I might develop a classification for sick, worried, and well parishioners and prospects.

A statement about the *subjects* of research may seem

elementary, but just before I wrote this, I was reviewing an elaborate research report in a psychiatric journal that did not tell me if the patients were hospitalized or walk-in clinic cases. To me that makes a great deal of difference in drawing conclusions about the results of a particular form of therapy, which was the purpose of the article.

But I didn't make an exact definition of my population, either. The eighty home or hospital visits included hospital visits to prospects. So, in defining the subjects, I would have to say that I included all persons with whom I had professional contact in one year.

Now that I had all the records of contacts for a year, what would I do with them? The next step would be some clear definition of procedure, some statement about methodology. The method was obviously field observation. I wanted to describe what I had learned about the condition of people whom I met in a first year of pastoral calling and counseling.

What would be the method of description? The categories of Boisen, described in the previous chapter, seemed most appropriate. But I added a category for prospects, persons whom I visited for no other reason than their need of Christ and his church. Also, I found records of talks with children, premarital counseling sessions, and visits to new couples expecting their first child. These seemed to fit into a separate category—the growing.

My final classification was more church-oriented, less problem-oriented, than Boisen:

Boisen	Southard
faithful	faithful
careless	careless
difficult	isolated
distressed	distressed

pagan	prospects
down and out[1]	growing[2]

I was careless in my classification. Definitions were loose; "regular and responsible in their church work" was all that I said about the faithful. I did add that there were some faithful counted only under the category of distressed. I would have done better to start with Boisen's definition: "Those who exhibit religious identification, a fair degree of discipline, readiness to cooperate, clear awareness of inconsistencies, and progressive unification." These five characteristics could have been the basis of inclusion in my category of faithful members. A more operational definition of each characteristic could have been given. And, what is most significant for research, I should have committed myself to the five characteristics and determined the operational definition, if possible, before I went through my own records of contacts.

What did I conclude from this loose classification and a tabulation of persons in each category? I noted that almost half of the persons contacted were either distressed (39 percent) or isolated (6 percent). Since I concentrated on routine home visitation and had personal contacts in the home, office, or hospital with 75 percent of the congregation in one year, I concluded that "about half of the church members had personal problems which were evident or which they were willing to discuss with me during my first year."[3]

There were many other conclusions in the article, but these would have to be considered as impressions rather than demonstrated evidence. For example, I recorded my temptation to consider a visit unsuccessful until I found some psychic or spiritual pathology in the parishioner. I decided that this expectation came from my earlier training as a chaplain in a mental hospital. Now I was learning that people could handle the crises of life in good health. My previous training gave me sensitivity to undercurrents of meaning and awareness of the relation of particular conversation to total life pattern. The pastorate changed my assumption that everyone should be sick in some way.

Although that is not a research conclusion in the sense that I presented evidence that others could examine, it was a useful conclusion for me to record. It committed me to a point of view that continued to be appropriate as a pastor. This is one of the personal and professional values of recording observations and drawing conclusions from them. You become more aware of what you are doing and can set a direction for ministry.

Choosing a Level of Research

My "homegrown" research should meet the criteria that John Tisdale set for 138 entries in *Pastoral Care and Counseling Abstracts, 1972:*

> Who the subjects of the research were
> What operations were carried out in reference to them
> What results ensued
> What conclusions were drawn.[4]

I say "should" because judgment depends on the level of research that is being undertaken. An exploration of routine pastoral records does not involve the design, conceptualization, and measurement that might be required in a doctoral project or a survey undertaken for a church agency. Expectations vary from graduate research to professional research to pastoral research. All can be classified as empirical if they produce evidence which another inquirer with different assumptions could understand and duplicate under similar circumstances. The difference lies in the time and attention that can be given to literature search, project design, data collection, processing, and analysis. There is no standard set of techniques or assumptions that separate graduate–professional–pastoral research. The questions that we will now consider about research are characteristic of all.

(1) Why Are You Searching?

If you don't have to satisfy anyone but yourself, you may meet minimum research requirements and satisfy your professional curiosity about the composition of a church membership and your acceptance by them as a counselor. But if you must satisfy a graduate committee, a sociology professor may challenge the restricted use of composition and require that you provide demographic data along with any psychological categories that you may wish to investigate. Whatever you are required to do, I hope that the motivation will basically follow that of Edwards, Boisen, and Oberlin. Out of their pastoral practice they saw questions that required objective study. Some of these were practical and operational, others were theoretical and a challenge to basic assumptions. My pastoral research in 1954 was practical (applied research), but I raised some questions about my assumptions of ministry (basic research).

In a doctor of ministry program, the field study encourages you to bring theory and practice together. If that is accomplished, the motivation for research has become a part of your self-concept as a professional person. The doing of theology, the practice of ministry, will include periodic examination of your assumptions, the production of evidence that you are accomplishing what you set out to do. The field requirement provides new adequacy for your continuing education, not only because of the techniques you learn, but also because of the motivation that is provided for continual reassessment. We might even base this kind of research on scripture! Paul proclaimed to the Corinthians that by an open statement of the truth he commended himself to them. How about some open statements of what you are doing, presented in a way that others can check with you the truth that you observe?

The depth of your study may be determined by the current state of the question. My motivation in 1954 was relatively uncomplicated. I was moving out of a pathological environment where every patient was supposed to be ill, and many staff talked of their personal neuroses or those of their colleagues. Now I was in a normal environment. What would I find there in the way of personal difficulties among the people whom I served?

If I had begun my pastorate in 1967, I might have been fascinated by a more complex issue, the "criterion problem" in religion. I would have devoted all my attention to Boisen's definition of the faithful as those who exhibit religious identification. Just what is that? Gerhard Lenski raised the question in *The Religious Factor* and Will Herberg in *Protestant, Catholic, Jew*. By 1967, an entire issue of the *Journal for the Scientific Study of Religion* was devoted to "the religious variable." Since then, two contributions to that Fall, 1967, issue have completed investigations of religion as a multidimensional aspect of behavior. I could have used Hunt and King's *Measuring Religious Dimensions* as a basis for religious identification if I had been born fifteen years later.[5]

(2) What Are You Looking For?

Research may start with a relatively uncomplicated survey of a new question or build on the accomplishments of others by using a refined questionnaire to delve into a specialized area. You can move in almost any direction if you commit yourself in the beginning to an answer to this question: What are you looking for?

You can often decide on the level of your study, if you are free to do so, by a survey of research literature on the question that interests you. The survey will often provide you with articles that define the problem in which you have interest, such as the work of King and Hunt on religious dimensions. Other monographs will explain designs used to pursue the problem and will tell you what results have been obtained and what questions are currently in need of investigation. On the basis of this search, you will often know if your modest or extensive investigation will be a contribution or not.

A listing of information service programs and agencies that are likely to have resources relevant to research studies has been compiled by David Moberg; Department of Sociology and Anthropology, Marquette University; Milwaukee, Wisconsin 53233. At the nominal cost of $1.95 researchers may obtain the International Directory of Religious Information Systems (1971) from Professor Moberg. It is updated through the quarterly *Adris Newsletter* of the Association for the Development of Religious Information Systems (ADRIS), which is also available from Professor Moberg, at $5.00 per volume, beginning in 1971 (back issues available).

The Research Department of the National Council of Churches; 475 Riverside Drive; New York, New York 10027 has maintained a library of studies on the church and society since the 1940s. A list of the classification of studies is available from the Research Department. Refer to the book and microfiche collection.

The *Review of Religious Research* is a quarterly journal of research on topics of interest to churches published by the RRA, annual meetings of which usually are held in conjunction with the Society for the Scientific Study of Religion, publisher of the *Journal for the Scientific Study of Religion.* Membership in both societies is open to ministers. I have found that attendance at the meetings and reading of the periodicals of these two societies is a major source of information on current research studies. Through personal contact with researchers at these meetings, I could obtain reports of studies which might not be reported in any literature or were reported only in summary form. Since the chairmanships and places of publication for both these societies change over a period of years, I would suggest writing to the research department of the National Council of Churches for current information on membership and subscriptions.

Major denominations are a source of information. They usually keep relevant studies which include information on research design, populations studied, and questions asked.

Information on Roman Catholic studies is available from the Glenmary Research Center, 4606 East-West Highway, Washington, D.C. 20014; from CARA, 1234 Massachusetts Avenue, N.W., Washington, D.C. 20005; and from the Departments of Sociology and Psychology of Catholic University and other Catholic institutions of higher education.

Southern Baptists, Methodists, United Presbyterians, and Lutherans have maintained research departments on modest budgets which do not permit extensive publication of findings. In some cases, an agency which requests a study from one of these departments will be reluctant to permit a minister to use the results in a published study. When you explain, however, that your desire is to obtain assistance in the development of your own research and promise that you will not refer to a specific study except by permission of the agency, the research department can usually obtain permission from the agency for you to inspect the study. Addresses and names of directors of research and planning are contained in the annual directories of each denomination.

A reference librarian will help you with the literature search. When he knows the areas of your interest, he may suggest such reference tools as *Psychological Abstracts, Abstracts for Social Workers, Sociological Abstracts, Index Medicus, Dissertation Abstracts International,* or Oscar Buros, *Mental Measurements Yearbook* (Highland Park, N. J.: Gryphon Press).

If your study is in the field of mental health, a major library will probably be part of Medline, a service of the National Library of Medicine. After determining the subject word on which references are to be requested, the librarian obtains a print-out from the computer terminal of recent periodical references on that topic. When you have seen the references, you may wish to request abstracts, which are available on selected articles.

Summaries of research studies are also available through professional organizations. For example, the Joint Council for Research and Pastoral Care and Counseling publishes an annual summary which is available from the Virginia Institute of Pastoral Care; 507 North Lombardy Street; Richmond, Virginia 23220.

The reading of related studies and correspondence with experienced persons should probably give you a sense of direction for your own study, a more precise statement of your objectives, a list of the most pertinent questions that should be asked, and a definition of the subject that you will pursue. This last item—definition—has been very troublesome in the area of religion. When a student writes, "We will look for signs of growth in the congregation through this program," just what are we looking for and how will we measure it? If you look at the studies of King and Hunt and the other articles for the *Journal for the Scientific Study of Religion* that have been mentioned earlier in this chapter, you will find some workable definitions within the area of religion. That is, you can describe a subject in terms which other people would understand and be able to measure along with you.

Another advantage of explicit definition is a limitation in the amount of time a minister must spend in collecting information and interpreting findings. By using a precise definition, you can shorten your survey and see that every question is related to the definitions you have defined. For example, you might take any one of the four patterns of church behavior defined in *The Fragmented Layman* by Thomas C. Campbell and Yoshio Fukuyama and use these as a basic measure of one phase of church participation. If you wish to define religion in terms beyond the church, the religious orientation scores of Allport could serve as basic descriptions of religiosity. These might be related, as in the study of Heidik, to specific populations such as hospital–nonhospital, young–old, or rural–urban.

It may be difficult to find a precise definition for an important term in your research study. Most of all, there is debate about the basic definition of religion. I like the thrust of Peter Berger's emphasis upon the experience of transcendence which he presented in a 1974 issue of the *Journal for the Scientific Study of Religion* (pp. 125-33). A definition that separates the sacred from the secular is often resisted, however, as by Nathan Grossman in the September, 1975, issue of the *Journal* (pp. 289-92).

(3) How Do You Look for Answers?

Once you have decided on a question that has meaning for you or your organization, you have to think about measurement. When I mention measurement, some people start looking for a test they can devise, distribute, and then count responses. That may be a part of your research design, but not necessarily. The question of measurement begins in an operational definition of "openhandedness." How do we present our observations in a way that other people can take hold of them, try them, see if they fit varying situations?

Openhandedness goes along with applicability. Is our method of measurement appropriate for the question we are studying? A sample survey will seem best for a one-time count of the opinions of people on a particular subject. Field observation would give us more realistic information on growth of religious consciousness. For example, there have been many sample surveys that counted the number of persons who had a definite conversion experience and those who identified their whole life as a part of God's will. But it would take observation like that of Edwards, Baxter, or Oberlin to say how people manifested their consciousness of God over a period of their life or during specific crises. If we picked out a particular crisis, such as bereavement, then a focused interview would be appropriate because it would probe the depth of feeling in a way that goes beyond the conventional questionnaire.

The varieties of research design are presented by Herbert Hyman in *Survey Design and Analysis* (Glencoe,

Ill.: Free Press, 1955) and by Earl Babbie in chapter 4 of *The Practice of Social Research* (Belmont, Cal.: Wadsworth Publishing Co., 1975). A companion to Babbie is *Practicing Social Research* by Robert Huitt, which offers extended activities on this type of research. If you plan to do interviewing, look at Hyman's *Interviewing in Social Research* (Chicago: University of Chicago Press, 1954).

There's always a danger of being intimidated and discouraged by the published reports of research based on a well-thought-out design. But you don't have to go as far with computers as Gerhard Lenski (*The Religious Factor*), Glock and Stark (*Religion and Tension in Society*), or Strommen (*A Study of Generations*) to see how these men think and what they do in the development of an inquiry. You might go back to the days before computers and read Boisen's *Exploration of the Inner World.* He told who his subjects were, how they were selected, what he looked for in their cases, and what he found. All this was part of a case history approach to research.

As an example of methodology, let's consider a more complex example than my 1954 field observation. When several experimental ministries were begun in Dallas, Texas, during 1967, the Presbyterian Board of National Ministries asked Marketing and Research Counselors, Inc. (MARC) to measure the changes in the awareness of and attitudes toward the benevolent activities of the Presbyterian Church in Dallas between 1967 and 1969.

To provide some measurement of awareness and attitudes, MARC developed a structured questionnaire. Interviews were conducted by a research team with every tenth person on the rolls of Presbyterian churches in the Dallas area. A quota was established for each church on the basis of the size of its membership. The questions were:

(1) First we would like for you to rate these types of organizations which devote all or part of their time and efforts to helping the underprivileged people of the city. You can rate these types or organizations easily by using the scale on this card. How about community organizations such as the United Fund, Salvation Army, and Goodwill Industries; how would you rate them on the first point————"Helps a lot of people?" [The card contained the following organizations: community, medical, civic, fraternal, churches in general, your denomination. The rating scale for each of these was: helps a lot of people, does very important work, tries hard to help, desires to help, does a lot on small budget, accomplishes a lot.]

(2) Are you a member of or do you contribute time to any of these type organizations? About how many hours a month do you spend on the average with this type organization? How many programs to help the underprivileged can you name that these organizations sponsor? [It was at this point that the researchers listened for any references to the experimental ministry programs that were beginning in Dallas, or any of the other social agencies that were sponsored by the church.]

(3) After writing down the programs that the respondent could name, the next question was, "Of the programs you mentioned above, which *one* do you believe is the most worthwhile?"

(4) "If you were going to increase the amount of time you spend with any of these types of organizations, which *one* would you select?"

(5) "Now I would like to read you the names of a few specific programs. Here is the first one." [The researcher then read off a list of church and community programs. This would be an additional check to the programs that were recalled in the previous questions.] After mentioning each program, the respondent was asked to tell whether or not he had heard of the program, what he thought the program was, who sponsored the program, and how he would rate the program on its usefulness to the community.

In both 1967 and 1969, respondents were asked to rate six types of organizations which devoted all or part of their time and efforts to helping the underprivileged. When comparisons were made between the two studies, it was found that the rating for the respondents' own denomination was higher in 1969 than in 1967.

An additional comparison was made between the ratings of men, women, and teen-agers. In 1969, adult women and teen-agers rated their own denomination higher than adult men on the six attitude points. Between 1967 and 1969, time reported with community medical and civic organizations increased, and average number of hours with the church decreased.

Awareness of Presbyterian programs increased from 18 to 28 percent between the two studies.

A Reminder

So far we have seen that there is no one way to conduct religious inquiry. But we do need to answer some questions:

Why did I undertake this study?

What question am I trying to answer?

What procedure do I use in the investigation?

When these questions are answered, we have committed ourselves to a definition of the problem and the major terms we will use in our search. Others will know just how we proceed so that they could do the same, either to replicate our findings or to find how the same questions operate in a different setting or with a different population.

Now we are ready to dig out and/or assemble the facts.

5. Digging Out the Facts

In the hills of north Georgia, Tom Conley sought material for his master of theology thesis on the mourners' bench. He not only had to find churches that were reported to practice a method developed by their spiritual ancestors in the second Great Awakening, he also had to convince local leaders that he was not a collector of bad debts for Sears and Roebuck or a scoffer of old-time religion from a "modernistic" seminary.

After conferences with courthouse and business leaders, he was recommended to a Thoreau-like inhabitant of a mountain cottage. This highly educated and reflective thinker was intrigued by the young theologian's search and told him who were the leaders of the mourners' bench revivals which were to begin in a week and how he was to gain their acceptance.

The main advice was, "Get in with the service. Be a part of everything." Mr. Conley followed this guidance by singing loudly in every service that he attended. In a small, wood-frame church, his voice was noted. By the third night of the revival, he was the singer who stood by the pulpit and led the congregation in the gospel songs that began the service and the invitational hymns that closed each meeting. As he later reported, this gave him the best possible opportunity to observe the mourners' bench, which was immediately before him, and the expressions of the congregation who were being urged to confess sin and come to the "anxious seat."

Start Where There Is Interest

The fortunate experience of Mr. Conley illustrates a goal of applied research: get as close as you can to the center of your subject for investigation. This dictum does not require you to be the center of things; that would certainly distort the investigation. Getting close means penetrating the interest of those who are observed or who give answers. What really matters to them? How do they interpret the issue you have begun to study?

How much responsibility will you take for what happens during and after your investigation? The more closely you penetrate the interest of your subjects, the more pressing is this question. One answer is informed consent. The subjects of the study or the authorities of an agency must be fully informed of the purpose and procedures of your inquiry.[1] If there is any possibility of inconvenience, injury, or indiscretion, this must be stated along with necessary assurances of protection against these hazards in relevant research. The greater the danger, the more rigorous must be the preparation. Subjects may be presented with a statement of purpose and procedures that they sign under the paragraph: "I understand the purposes and procedures, and give my consent to participate. I agree to release of data and findings under the conditions stated above (previous paragraphs)."

This precaution is routine in medical research, but might not be necessary in many religious studies. What is usually more important in religious inquiry is a guarantee of anonymity. How will the individual or agency be protected against undesirable publicity? (If this cannot be avoided—or is desired—this is agreed to from the beginning.) Usually, a researcher will obscure identifying details of individuals if he uses personal interviews. If a questionnaire is used, the personal address is given a number and the list of addresses is locked up. The numbers appear in some inconspicuous place on the questionnaire that is to be returned. This allows the researcher to know if he has gained a representative return (for example, if pastor subjects are listed as numbers 1-50, lay leaders as 51-100, and denominational officials 101-150, a check of the number on returned questionnaires will answer the question of representation).

In one questionnaire study, the identifying number was on the return envelope under the postage stamp which was loosely attached. As the research assistant pulled off the stamp from one return, she found the number obliterated with black ink and "boo!" scratched in.

The gaining of informed consent is almost automatic in studies conducted by a pastor with his people concerning a mutual problem. When Clarence Drummond told the adult and youth departments of his Sunday school that he wished to distribute a questionnaire "to help us understand the ministry that our people really want in a changing [racially] neighborhood, and to help me with my doctor of ministry studies," 90 percent of the questionnaires were filled out and returned after the worship service.[2]

If the survey is to include a number of churches or agencies, officials should be contacted and asked for support in explaining the study to subjects whom the authorities may recommend for participation in the project. In a study of the impact of religious TV, pastors asked a young people's group and men and women's Bible classes to view video tapes and write down their reactions "so that our denomination will know how people of various ages respond to the subject matter."

No deception is ethical in explanations of inquiries, and all subjects have the right to check conclusions that the researcher makes about them as individuals. If the study is by questionnaire, each subject should be offered a copy of the conclusions of the study, if he desires them.

Informed consent not only starts the research, it also adds to the completeness of a survey. The 90 percent return for Mr. Drummond is several times the amount with which many graduate students content themselves in obtaining a sample (although they are aided by various statistical procedures and survey methods to determine the representative nature of their sample).

When we start where people are interested, the sample will usually be adequate and there will be few refusals. In contrast, resistance may be high when people do not think that we have their interests in mind. When Mr. Drummond and church leaders took a community-interest questionnaire to blacks who had recently moved into the neighborhood of the church, only 14 out of 194 questionnaires were returned, even though the questionnaire itself had been constructed by a black consultant.[3]

What happens when you need more response from a resistant or indifferent population? You might rethink the relevance of your study or the way you approach the problem. And how about the way you approach people? Middle-class whites may not win the interest of new blacks in their area. Why not employ some black students from a high school or community college to explain the purpose of the questionnaire to neighborhood blacks? Also, there are many persons who do not read well or resist forms to be filled out. Let the students read the questions and write in the answers.

A high response can be obtained if a group learns that surveys are being used to actively help them solve a besetting problem. Mr. Drummond used the results of his first church survey during a series of seminars for church leaders and members. Leaders stated that the question-naire itself aided their own self-examination. The presentation of results also helped them to see what people really thought about shifting, emotionally ladened issues. When a second church survey was taken a year later from the same Sunday school group, the returns were 100 percent.

When the inquiry taps current interest, leaders will assist the researcher in collecting results and interpreting findings. The group leader of a hospital visitation team aided her pastor in the content analysis of letters of appreciation from out-of-town patients who were visited by team members. She not only collected the pool of items from letters that formed the main subjects for an evaluation questionnaire, she also saw that the evaluation questionnaire was filled out by every team member. She explained, "It's done me so much good to see just how we helped these people; we'll have a stronger ministry when we really know what we are doing."

When the people who face a problem become a part of the research effort, they usually use the results to guide their actions. Leaders in Mr. Drummond's church used the church opinion survey, a survey of the actions of other churches in transitional neighborhoods, and a study of key biblical passages to guide them toward a relevant community program under church sponsorship. It was clear from the second opinion survey that the church did not wish to relocate and that a continued emphasis should be placed on emergency food and clothing services, supervised recreation for community children, and statements in all literature that people of all races were welcomed to the church. The leaders still were bothered by the question, "Why don't they want to come to our church?" That had not been a part of either survey.

Research that begins with the subjects' interests and builds on the mutual responsibilities of researcher and group leaders will often become the basis of relevant action. But the group may be frustrated because the study did not answer a vexing question like, "Why don't they want to come to our church?" Personal interviews or surveys of black leaders, for example, would produce more answers than the paper questionnaires distributed door to door.

Who Will Answer?

Getting started on our research will involve both the acceptability of our research proposal to the people involved and a procedure for getting the answers that are of interest to us.

We could keep our study at an uncomplicated level by looking at all the records that we had as a pastor with people during a year or asking all the people in church on a given Sunday to fill out our questionnaire. That solves the sampling problem, so long as we are careful to state in any conclusion that it is based on that limited population. We are making no attempt to obtain a representative sample of all the community; our information relates only to those contacted by a pastor or those who are in church on one Sunday (which might be 40 percent of the population in a "God-fearing" community). We are not to generalize in a way that would implicate the other 60 percent of the town. Also, we cannot expand our conclusions to take in all members of our denomination; the study is limited to those we contact.

Some subjects may be broader than one church or one section of town. If such is our interest, we must consider more complicated issues of sampling, as occurred when a doctor of ministry student proposed a study of the characteristics of church leadership in his state.

When a research consultant in sociology was asked to comment on the proposal, he made the following observations: (1) The questionnaire does not ask for identification as church officer, members who are not officers, or pastors. No information is called for by sex, although age, education, and income are included in the questionnaire. If each of these characteristics of the sample has been found to be significant in opinions of people about the church and its work, they should be distinguished. (2) The use of local churches as a basic unit for the sampling is appropriate, but ten questionnaires in each church would not be enough for comparisons to be made on the basis of the categories that have just been suggested. The graduate student should increase the size of his sample in individual congregations and reduce the number of churches in which he is seeking to obtain information. (3) The manner of selecting respondents in each congregation has not been specified. Will it be done by the pastor? If so, what will be his criteria for selection? In many cases, a pastor would select persons who were readily available and free to fill out questionnaires or those who would reflect what the pastor or some other official in the church would consider to be a representative view. (4) The student may not wish to use all of the categories that have been suggested, such as sex, age, education, church officer–nonofficer. But he should include the very significant category of active–inactive.

The questions of the consultant are aimed at a major objective of sampling, which is to provide a sufficient size to make a study sensitive to real differences on the subject under consideration. Since the amount of money as well as the time of a researcher is limited, he must choose between a variety of sampling methods that will provide him with maximum sensitivity to differences with a minimum size of sample population.

If you are interested in opinions (on two or three questions) from an entire denomination in one town or city, you would probably choose a simple random-sample method. This would allow you to state with confidence that your findings from two hundred persons in a sample would represent the opinions of the overwhelming majority of persons in the city who are members of that denomination. You have this confidence because the random-sampling technique provides the possibility that every person of a particular denomination in this city has an equal chance of being part of the sample.

How do you make sure that each member of the denomination has an equal chance? In a study of the opinions of Presbyterians concerning race and social class in one city, every fifth church in the presbytery was asked to cooperate in the study. If a church refused to participate in the study, than a church in the same social economic strata and size was requested to participate in the study. (Socioeconomic characteristics of a town or region may usually be obtained from a local planning and development office or from some sociology thesis in a neighboring college.)

In each church, a random sample was drawn from the rolls of active and inactive members. From a table of random numbers (which is usually in the appendix of any book of statistics) a number was drawn. This might be number six, which would mean that the sample would start with the sixth person on the church roll. To obtain a sample of two hundred persons, it was determined that every tenth person after the first random number would be selected for interviewing. When the list was complete, volunteers from each church and some graduate students from a neighboring university were used to conduct the interviews. A control group was obtained by interviewing the nearest neighbor, beginning with the person who lived to the right of the respondent, if houses were of equal distance from one another.

One of the major problems of simple random-sampling is nonrespondence. One of the reasons for the use of graduate students was to provide someone who could be at a home when it was known that the respondent was there. This may seem to be an elemental precaution, but it has been missed in many surveys. For example, studies of the attitudes of minority groups toward police have often been drawn from interviews during the day with minority groups who happen to be at home when the government officials were in the neighborhood. When some of the same questions were asked of persons who were home in the evening, it was found that the working husbands and wives, who did not get home until five or six P.M., were eager for more police protection and ascribed more brutality to the unemployed people who were home during the day than they did to the police who occasionally patrolled on their block.

The problem of representativeness can also be solved by a stratified random sample. This second method of sampling is obtained by separating the population into strata, such as the characteristics by income, and then selecting a simple random sample from each of the strata.

The stratified random method will provide more homogeneous data within each strata than in the population as a whole. More attention can be drawn to the characteristics of each stratum and comparisons made between strata.

The strata may be degree of loyalty to the church.

Sociologist Joseph Fichter categorized persons in one community who 'had been baptized as Roman Catholics into the following groupings: nuclear members, who are the most active participants and presumably the most faithful; modal members, who normally practice their religion but are not very enthusiastic; marginal members, who conform to the bare minimum of yearly confession and attendance at the mass and expect their children to be baptized as Catholic; and dormant members, who have given up the practice of their religion but have not joined another denomination.

Michael York asked the pastors of one hundred Presbyterian churches to list two adults in each of these categories and two youths among modal members and two among marginal members. The pastors were also asked to name two nonchurch-related adults. A description of the characteristics of each class was provided to the pastor. He was asked to invite the persons whom he had chosen to participate in the survey without indicating their classification.

This method of sampling was particularly useful in the attitude survey that followed on aspects of church life. The nuclear adults were most responsive in answering the survey, especially those in urban churches of moderate size. Dormant members were much more responsive from the smaller churches. Twenty-one percent of the total survey sample turned out to be modal youth from large urban churches.

A pastor or graduate student may find that he does not have time or money for a study of one hundred churches, or even of two hundred persons in an entire city. The answer to this problem may be a third type of sample, the cluster. A common cluster would be one section of a city which is defined through some demographic survey as representing a particular socioeconomic group or other characteristics, such as Polish-American. Or the pastor may draw upon a previous study, such as the one of Dr. York, to follow up with an analysis of questions already presented to the modal members of the York study or additional questions to that strata of his survey.

The nonrespondents in the York survey were sent a second letter and then were called to ask for their answers on a few of the crucial questions in the survey. By comparing their answers to five questions with those of persons who responded more readily, the researcher would know if he had really tapped the entire denomination or just received answers from those who were favorable to his point of view.[4]

If your study will involve some questions of sampling design, questionnaire construction, distribution, and follow-up, I would suggest chapters 5-8 of Earl Babbie's *Survey Research Methods* (Belmont, Cal.: Wadsworth Publishing Co., 1973) or his *Practice of Social Research*, chapters 5-11 (Belmont, Cal.: Wadsworth Publishing Co., 1975).

After we know what we want to ask and who we want to ask, we have to put ourselves into the position of the respondent and say, "Now how does this question sound to me?" Only when we know that the respondents understand our meaning and are encouraged to give their authentic answer, can we say that our study really demonstrates what we designed it to do. This is called validity, and may take much ingenuity and patience to achieve, as we will see in some of the following studies.

Are People Answering the Right Question?

A chaplain resident in research asked for opinions about religion from one hundred hospitalized patients, eighty-four of whom were long-term residents of a central state hospital. A control group of forty-seven first-year theological students and thirty-three adults in Sunday school classes were also asked the same questions. The data was analyzed by the principle components method of factor analysis. That is, all of the answers were run through a computer to see which ones were associated with one another. It was found, for example, that twenty-five of the answers were commonly given by persons with the lowest education. These persons were usually patients. The twenty-five answers had the common characteristic of a religious mood of failure, guilt, and feelings that God was punishing and angry. The factor analysis was the way of boiling down the many answers into a small set of more general characteristics, or factors. The "primordial God" factor of twenty-five answers was one of the seven in the study.

When a consultant looked over this study he wrote, "Your control sample was chosen so casually that nonpatient status was confounded with education and church involvement." The majority of the control group were highly educated persons who were regular in their church attendance. The majority of the patient group were not so frequent in their church attendance and had grade school or some high school education.

In his original conclusion, the chaplain thought that he was isolating a characteristic of religious thinking among psychiatric patients when he saw the primordial God factor. This would have been consistent with the psychoanalytic interpretation of religion among the mentally ill. But, as he saw from the consultant's report, he was actually measuring opinions about religion among a poorly educated group of persons who were seldom in church.[5]

"Am I really asking questions that are related to the question that is in my mind?" This is one of the problems of validity which the chaplain faced. By noticing the difference in education between the patient and nonpatient population, he could prepare a more valid instrument in which questions were more related to mental illness than to social class. This would be done by comparing hospitalized and nonhospitalized persons of the same socioeconomic stratum. John Gleason did this at a central state hospital and found that 87 percent of the nonpatients disagreed with the statement "I try to avoid pain and sorrow at all cost," whereas 41 percent of the patients disagreed. Chaplain Gleason found several other statements about religion, ethics, or world view in which there were statistically significant differences between patients and nonpatients. Once these statements had been identified, we could know that persons who answer them in a certain way will be similar to or different from the thinking of persons who are actively psychotic. We may not know the reason for the connection between psychiatric diagnosis and world view, but we will know that there is a connection. Since these questions seem to measure something that is characteristic of a particular population, we would say that they are valid.

Another question of validity is, "Does the person understand what I am asking?" This does not mean that he understands our hypothesis or the characteristic that we are seeking to identify through a range of questions, but it does mean that he knows what we are after through this particular question or statement.

Questions concerning religion are especially prone to contamination of variables because religion is such a global subject. ("Contamination of variables" would be the confusion of education and church attendance with religious world view.) We can increase validity by deciding if we are asking about attitudes toward religious institutions or inner devotional attitudes. James Dittes has characterized the first as "outside" studies of religion in which the usual questions are about institutional affiliation and belief in God. In contrast, "inside" questions have been developed by Kline and Richards, King, Allen and Spilka, Allport, Campbell and Fukuyama. These internal measures will identify those persons who take the worship of God seriously. The internal measures would have a higher validity than the outside measures which are generally characterized as "favorable attitude for organized religion." [6]

A third part of validity is: "Are people responding as they are really known by others or just as they see themselves?" Clergymen are often naïve about this question. They devise questionnaires in which people can give obvious answers which are motivated by a desire for social approval. This will measure what people think of themselves, but will provide less reliable evidence of how other people interpret them.

One guard against this tendency to give socially acceptable answers was developed by Liston Mills in his doctoral thesis on the stability of converts in their religious profession. One year after their signing of a decision card, converts were asked what the revival had meant to them. They were asked to give the name of a friend or relative who could provide some evaluation of the revival's impact upon the decision-maker. In some instances the friend or relative saw the change or lack of change as the convert did. In other cases the relative saw something different, as in the case of wives who commented on the consideration that their husbands now showed to them about family purchases, whereas the husbands did not mention this in their interviews with Mr. Mills. Also, children often reported that none of their friends knew that they had joined the church, so they could give no name of a person who could tell about their change or conversion.

Another measure of validity is the internal consistency of answers to questions about religion. Victor Kline and James Richards, Jr., interviewed a cross section of adults in Salt Lake City to establish some correlations between overall religiosity or religious commitment and such variables as male–female, love and compassion, church attendance, and frequency of prayer. They found no correlation between the major religiosity factors such as high church attendance and frequency of prayer, with such variables as "having love and compassion for one's fellowman" or "possessing humility." [7]

Who Will Believe My Report?

The findings of researchers like Kline and Richards are controversial. People with different assumptions will question their conclusions. Those who agree will want to know that they really understand what has been said and why. People are looking for objectivity, especially in a report on a subjective area such as values and religious beliefs.

I visualize objectivity as the ability to stand beside another observer and show him a subject of interest to us in such a way that he can identify what we see. This characteristic of research will be increased when we are able to do at least three things.

First, we can conduct a "pretest" with subjects who are likely to agree with us and with some who would not. If the test is confusing to respondents and if the results seem to have no significance to those who rate them, there must be some lack of clarity in our perception of the problem and ability to tell others what we are looking for. The open-ended questions of Dr. York might be considered as a large scale pretest that would reduce the suggestive bias of denominational officials by giving them the actual thinking of representative church members about denominational programs.

A second increase in objectivity comes through attention to our interviews with subjects, if this is called for by our research design. We begin with some decision about the nature of the data that we wish to report. Is it material that can only be found by the active involvement of the interviewer in the relationship with a subject? If so, we will have a general frame of reference for our interview, but will not expect it to be conducted within the strict limits of prearranged questions. On the other hand, we may want information about types of activities or the number of times that a person has engaged in them. Relationships might not be as significant, and we could increase reliability by giving our subjects the questions printed on cards, to which they could respond.

We can check on our impressions and observations from interviews with a questionnaire to the same subjects. This was the method adopted by Robert Bermudes, who spoke as a pastor with the wives of submarine crewmen and then tested his observations with a questionnaire about the stages of grief.

Most of all, we can check on our interviews by asking a panel of judges to score our observations to see if others will agree with what we have concluded. This is actually the third control for objectivity, the reliability of ratings between judges.

Russell Allen and Bernard Spilka developed their interviews on committed and consensual religion with a definition of five cognitive components, within which they would differentiate between committed and consensual:

Content: abstract–relational versus concrete–literal;

Clarity: discerning versus vague;

Complexity: differentiated versus monopolistic;

Flexibility: candid and open versus restrictive and nonaccessible;

Importance: relevant versus detached–neutral.[8]

A definition of each of these terms was explained to four psychology faculty members who were then trained for four hours through illustrations and exercises to rate the consensual and committed orientations. Practice interview tapes, similar to those which were used in the actual investigation, were the basis for the ratings.

Seven of the interviews from the research were then rated by the faculty members. There was an 86 percent agreement between the four raters on the seventy possible comparisons. This provided the researchers with some assurance that they had described their observations in terms that others could understand and utilize.

Are Our Answers Consistent?

The inter-rater reliability for Allen and Spilka involved 70 possible comparisons for each cognitive component and a total of 420 comparisons for all the components. If the judges had continued their comparisons for all of the tapes in the study (71), how much agreement would we expect?

The estimated reliability of judgments across categories, .93, was obtained from an analysis of variance technique. It is a measure of the amount of difference of opinions between judges if they were to continue to make comparisons on seventy-one different tapes, instead of just seven. The procedure saves us the time and money of asking for judgments on seventy-one tapes, and summarizes a mass of statistical data in a logical content.

A knowledge of statistical manipulations and access to a computer are required to save this time and money. Since this is beyond the training of most clergymen, it is time to call in a consultant who will tell us if some statistical studies are necessary to show the consistency of our measurements. If so, he can suggest appropriate procedures and contract for computer time, if necessary.

During our conversations with the consultant, he will probably explain that much of his work is to check on the possibility of errors by chance. If we want to know more of what he is talking about, or if we want to do some of the statistical operations ourselves, we might read Linton Freeman's *Elementary Applied Statistics* (New York: John Wiley & Sons, 1968).

At the most basic level, Celeste McCollough and Loche Van Atta have provided a programmed text, *Statistical Concepts* (New York: McGraw-Hill Book Co., 1963).

After you have grasped some of the concepts, *Statistics: A Guide to the Unknown* (San Francisco: Holden-Day, 1972) by Judith Tanur will show how statistics have been used in a variety of practical problems of research.

More advanced texts are Quin McNemar's *Psychological Statistics* (New York: John Wiley & Sons, 1969), and Allen L. Edwards' *Experimental Design in Psychological Research* (New York: Holt, Rinehart and Winston, 1968).

A Review

When you're ready to dig out the data, discover how people feel about your inquiries into their lives or surroundings. They may be very cooperative if you ask for their assistance. Place yourself in their way of thinking. How do they understand what you are asking?

Then draw back a little from the problem and look at the area of investigation. Are you asking questions or participating in an observation that is representative enough for you to draw some general conclusions? Take some time to develop a sample or a technique for asking questions that is both typical and comprehensive. While you are doing some thinking, you can try out your method of investigation with a representative group of respondents. If this pretest shows that people comprehend and are cooperative with your investigation, you're ready for a larger survey.

Of course, your study may be more case-oriented or it may be a focused interview. You still need to know if people can identify what you're getting at, but you won't need to get at so many different people. Instead, the problem will be more deep than wide. How will you define the issues you investigate so others will be able to follow? Can you find reliable people who will help control your bias by making judgment of the data with you? The more you know about a few people, the more important is objectivity.

One way to increase objectivity is through some statistical techniques which should increase the certainty of your findings by measuring the possibility of errors due to chance in your computations.

I do not want too much emphasis on control and objectivity, even though we need more of this in religious research. If we push our well-designed processes upon our experimental group for a long period of time, we may end up with the bothersome side effect that has been labeled Hawthorne Effect, after the Hawthorne plants in which the work of women was measured after a series of changes in lighting, longer rest pauses, and better incentive plans. Productivity did go up. But when the experimenters conducted the same tests under the original conditions of poor lighting, short rest pauses, and no incentive plans, they also found improved production. The attention of the researchers had proved enough incentive by itself for increased performance.

Our problem, then, is to provide some controls over our observations without calling so much attention to what we are doing that the situation is unnatural or extraordinary.[9]

6. Explaining Our Findings

Facts do not speak for themselves. They are inert pieces of data which do not move us to understanding until they are associated with the assumptions that lie behind them and the purposes toward which they may be directed. A fact speaks in relationship, first to that which caused us to hunt for it (assumptions), and second to that which justifies our search (goal or purpose).

Fitting facts together is usually a process of (1) categories, (2) comparisons, and (3) correlations. These are logical operations of our daily life as we solve problems. First, we describe what we see in terms that others will quickly understand. The category must identify a person, place, or thing in such a way that a related person, place, or thing is not confused with it. During the Crimean War a courier told an officer of the light brigade to take the guns on "that hill," and six hundred men thundered down a valley toward *another* hill and were decimated. Much research has gone the same way.

After some trial and error with independent judges you should have confidence that your categories will not be confused and the definitions fit. Then it is natural to see the difference between a mountain and a molehill of evidence. How does this finding compare to that one? It's a question of more and less. That sounds straightforward, but there's a catch, as we will see in the example from Chaplain Gleason's research. We must compare categories that are on a scale that may read more or less, lower class–higher class, or any other statements of preference that vary from person to person or day to day. We do not compare that which moves (more or less) with that which is fixed (sex, place of birth, denomination). It would be like the oft-told mistake of the college freshman who saw a blank by the word "sex" on his entrance form and wrote in "sometimes."

When we show that our categories identify preferences of people that can be measured against each other (for example, pessimistic versus optimistic patients or church members), then we want to know "why?" This is the question of correlation. With much ingenuity and resources you may move all the way from description to correlation; but with limited time and resources, you may be content with discrete (clearly separated) descriptions, or perhaps with some comparisons. That's quite adequate research, especially when it is difficult to formulate queries that will really discriminate preferences. So, be content with any part of the who-what-why process as you read the following examples, which show that clergymen can get started, even though they sometimes get stuck.

Categories: Two Views of Description

Explanation begins in a description of what we have observed or reports of what others have observed. Here we have two viewpoints, that of the persons who report their observations to a researcher and that of the researcher who describes these persons and their observations and who may add his own descriptions to those of others.

The distinction between these two views is sometimes blurred in research by ministers. In an address entitled "How Do You Measure God?" John Tisdale noted that in most research articles the definition of individual religiosity is either implicit or derived from measures developed by the researcher himself. We do not know how the individual viewed himself as a religious person.

An attempt to clarify the individual's perception of religion was made by Jackson Carroll and Gerald Jenkins at the Georgia Mental Health Institute. In extended interviews, patients were asked open-ended questions which would evoke responses in the following categories: (1) significant relationship with others, (2) important groups to which you belong or aspire to, (3) important decisions made in life, (4) significant events or experiences, (5) embarrassing moments, (5) very good experiences, (7) serious temptations, (8) values or philosophy of life, (9) what you would wish for if you had three wishes, (10) what you would change from the past or hope for the future, (11) questions about religious concepts and participation.[1]

Case histories were developed from the chaplain's notes on these eleven categories. The case history was followed by inferences on self-concept, world view, and ultimate concern. This method allowed distinctions to be known between the inferences of an interviewer or researcher and the statements of a patient about his own religious commitment.

The patients were actually explaining the meaning of religion to themselves in the descriptions that were evoked through the eleven categories. This would certainly be a pleasing method of research for pastors, since it enables a person to explain religious feelings to himself and to the minister who interviews him.

In the case history approach, qualitative differences were not prominent. Neither the patient nor the chaplain had to rate degree of significance for statements made in any of the categories. The research was designed to produce a gestalt, a comprehensive view of religion in the life of an individual.

But what if we are describing a more discrete aspect of religion or feelings about the self? Then our explanations will hinge upon an ability to ascribe a variety of responses to a single category or subject. The series of descriptions should enable our subject and other researchers to see the differences in degree of religious commitment (consensual–committed) or psychological mood (optimistic–pessimistic).

John Gleason, James Travis, and John Sharp sought to distinguish the mood or mind-set of patients at a central state hospital. Forty-two patients were given four statements and asked for their interpretation or explanation of the statements. The statements had been selected during a pilot study in which more than a hundred statements were given to patients and nonpatients. These four statements were answered affirmatively more often by patients than nonpatients: (1) I believe we are living in the last days of the world; (2) Suicide is an unforgiveable sin; (3) The human mind is the highest intelligence in the universe; (4) I try to avoid pain and sorrow at all costs.

After receiving the written (or oral) comments on each statement, the chaplains asked a series of questions on the religious history of the patient.

This completed the first step in the study, the gathering of information. But now that the data had been gathered, how was it to be assembled? To describe the significance of religion among forty-two patients, we must extract that which seems significant out of each history and then arrange these separate pieces of the histories into categories. The label for each category will be a symbol of similarity among all the statements gathered under it.

The assembling of statements under separate categories

was done by two clinical chaplains, one psychiatrist, one psychology technician, and one social worker. After three one-hour discussion periods, the raters agreed on categories such as the following:

Outlook for the future: This refers to the individual's expectations about things to come, the basic stance in anticipation of future events. (a) Pessimistic: expressions of hopelessness; an attitude of being resigned to the blows to be meted out by Fate and/or God; (b) Optimistic: expressions of hope; an attitude that things will be better, that God cares, that the future holds opportunity.

Other categories were: ideation, denial, despair, judgment, relationships, God, responsibility, significance of religion.

The Problem of Comparison

Once we have identified the categories under which a group of findings may be classified, we are ready for the next step in interpretation, which is comparison between categories. In Gleason's study, each of the raters was given the forty-two religious histories and the answers of the forty-two patients to the four statements (such as, "I believe we are living in the last days of the world"). The patients had rated each of the four statements: strongly agree, agree, undecided, disagree, strongly disagree.

The raters were to read each history and decide if the patient were pessimistic or optimistic, concrete or abstract in thinking—and so on through the opposites that characterized each of the nine categories of the religious history. On a tally sheet, a rater would check *A* under category 1 if he thought a patient's outlook to the future were pessimistic, or B if he thought it were optimistic.

When each rater had completed his work, the percentage of agreement was calculated by dividing the number of disagreements of raters on one category by the largest possible number of disagreements. Since raters could disagree on both A and B under each category, the total would be eighty-four. This percentage was substracted from 100 percent to arrive at the percentage of agreement. In category 1, for example, there were nineteen unanimous agreements, or 59.5 percent.

The next step was to compare the ratings of each patient (optimistic–pessimistic, etc.), with the agreement or disagreement of each patient on the four statements (world coming to an end, etc.). But when Chaplain Gleason looked at the ratings on category 1 relating to the patient's outlook for the future, he found thirty-eight As (pessimistic) and three Bs (optimistic). There was not enough variability in this category for comparisons to be made with the four statements.

After looking at this problem with Chaplain Gleason, James Dittes suggested that the raters make finer distinctions between optimism and pessimism, such as strongly pessimistic, moderately pessimistic, and so forth. Or, the raters might concentrate on specific sections in each case history rather than ranging over the entire history. Precision might increase discrimination between optimistic and pessimistic.

Why this insistence upon demonstration of opposites? Isn't it enough to find that patients are pessimistic? Yes, if our study is limited to description. But if we are trying to explain pessimism, we must tear it apart, get inside the thinking of the patient, look at his interpretation of issues from varying points in his life. Is he pessimistic about everything—all the time—with every one? When we begin to find specifics, we find differences, and these differences become the basis of comparisons within the life of the patient, between patients, and between patients and other populations.[2]

Correlations: What, How, and Why

When we have developed categories that are different enough from one another for comparisons to be made, we have moved from "what" to "how." We can now begin to see how one fact operates in relation to other facts. Does it appear with this one or that one, and under what conditions? For example, when we have established clear ratings of pessimistic and optimistic among mental patients, will pessimism tend to appear in the case histories of those who think the end of the world is near, or will the latter thought be more frequent among those who are optimistic—or both?

Correlation is the process by which we discover if this fact is related to that fact. The process usually begins in the establishment of some association between phenomena we observe. Do we usually find that people who are regular in church attendance are also for (or against) government subsidies for housing and civil rights legislation? If so, there must be some relationship, but how is it to be explained?

The question of how facts are related to each other is another step in comparisons. We could stop with the simple explanation that church people are prejudiced. Or we could go on to make some other associations. What does church attendance mean to the individual? This gets at the question of "why." When this is done through such tests as intrinsic–extrinsic or consensual and committed, we find that the conventional member looks for security both in the church and in other social relationships. His need for security explains both his outward piety and his prejudice.[3]

Since ministers tend toward purposive explanations, it is easy for us to jump from statistical evidence of correlation to the conclusions that one fact has caused another. After all, we are trained to lead people toward goals in life. Why shouldn't we look for reasons, assign motivation to attitudes and actions that correlate closely with each other?

Well, what will you do with the well-known statistical association between ministers' salaries and liquor consumption?[4] Which is cause and which is effect?

We would be on safer ground to look for some independent variable that moves such disparate (we assume) data as size of clergy income and consumption of strong drink. This search for additional, and hopefully explanatory, variables is one answer to the question of causality. If we can find one fact that does explain others, then we can begin to talk about motivation. Robert Mitchell found that middle-aged ministers reported more frequent counseling of parishioners than older or younger ministers. Why? He sought an answer through depth personal interviews with some clergy and through a review of literature, in which he found the Lynn, Massachusetts, study that ministers tend to communicate with persons close to them in age. He concluded, "If this is true in general, then the oldest ministers lack parishioners older than themselves, while younger ministers lack adult parishioners younger than they are. Middle-aged ministers have the largest reservoir of potential clients, since they have parishioners both older and younger than themselves."[5]

We will not really know if Mitchell is correct until someone else has taken this part of his study and expanded on the information: (1) What are the percentages of parishioners in the age ranges of under-35, 35–44, 45–54,

55 and over? This will be a check on possibility for counsel across ages. (2) What age persons do consult the minister, and with what types of problems? This will give us a clue to motivation for counseling as it is related to age of the minister. Other questions could be answered from data that Mitchell collected but did not relate to frequency of counseling. What is the size of the church, and how involved is the pastor in administrative activities?

It takes one study after another to assign meaning to the facts that we have obtained through research. Usually this is a progression from "what" to "how" to "why."

"What" is an explanation if it describes a fact more lucidly and graphically than it was known before. Studies of outcome of training in community mental health are not very convincing when they concentrate on changes in attitudes. But when questions are asked about new contacts with other agencies or with ministers, juvenile court workers, and so forth, the training seems to have some durable results. If the "what" is describable, measurable, and reportable, then progress has been made toward explanation. The explanation of community mental health training would be that professionals who already have motivation to work in the community will learn of more agencies with which they can work, the way in which this can be done, and the people who have already done it.[6]

The question of "how" will show that facts function in relation to one another in sequence or under specified conditions or both. The states of grief described by Dr. Lindemann in the 1940s have been a useful explanation for pastors of the grief process. It doesn't tell why, but it does allow us to predict what will come next, so that we can prepare ourselves and others. In the very explanation of what usually happens, we bring comfort.

Sequence is one type of explanation. The specification of significant conditions is a related type. Exploratory research by clergy will often identify the forces that facilitated or inhibited a project, even though these were not clearly known when the study began. In a study of the chaplain as a change agent and as an educator of change agents, Ed Thornton found that other professionals were more active, dominant, or abrasive than the chaplains. But the impact of the project was significant in showing the project director some different ways of strategizing, demonstrating the power of video-teaching, changing seminary curricula, and bringing chaplains of an area closer together.[7]

The "why" of a correlation will lead beyond explanation to interpretation. We trace the relation of the facts we have observed to some general law of nature, concept of society, or axiom of theology. The fact and its function are now set in the broad picture of meaning. That is, the significance of this act or attitude is shown by its movement toward some goal and its associations with other acts and attitudes which have value.[8]

The Concept of the Classical

We have interpreted an observation or category when we can show its relationship to our assumptions and to our goal or purpose for the study. But what are the assumptions, goals, purposes that guide our research description, selection, and presentation? In religious research we usually have a concept of that which is most desirable, the model for all those who think or believe as we do about a particular subject or who are identified with a specific religious group. It is from this edifying and typical person or pronouncement that we mold our assumptions and set our goals. We formulate the model by asking: "What is most essential? What is most typical? What is most attractive to those who believe as I do, or to those whom I am studying?"

Joachim Wach has called for a "concept of the classical" in the study of religions.[9] This is a way for facts to be abstracted out of a mass of observations and set in a structure of value to a culture. It is possible in religious studies when we continually look for the whole that is greater than the parts that we have isolated, observed, and correlated.

An illustration of the value of the classical is Gibson Winter's criticism of Gerhard Lenski's definition of religion in *The Religious Factor*. In that book, Lenski isolates one dimension of religion, commitment, and concentrates upon the subjective meaning of this term. He does not, as Winter observes, ask about the content that goes with commitment. In classical terms, we would insist on commitment to something. Or, as Bishop Temple once wrote, the purpose of an open mind is to close on something.

The intentional structure of religion is ignored in a subjective study. We do not know what people think of the God to which they are committed. As Winter notes, this lack in religious studies may have resulted from Paul Tillich's emphasis upon ultimate concern. The object of faith is less significant than the feeling of concern.[10]

Among social scientists, the concept of the classical has been applied to religion by Max Weber. As W. Widich Schroeder once observed, Weber solved the part–whole problem with his ideal types. The nonrepeatable ideal type illustrated one way of dealing with a special whole whose constituent parts were unlikely to emerge again in a similar configuration. At the same time, his repeatable ideal type illustrated a way of dealing with the common and universal components of human experience. In his book with Victor Obenhaus, *Religion in American Culture*, Schroeder used many open-ended questions in interviews and encouraged interviewers to probe and rephrase questions. This led to more emphasis upon dynamics and creativity in explanation, and less emphasis upon statistical abstractions or excessive causal analysis. This seemed to be a most appropriate methodology in a study of religious experience, which the authors defined as the sensitive and harmonious unification of causal and conceptual facets of human experience.

The concept of classical allows an interpretation of that which is characteristic by that which is normative. We measure that which *is* (so far as we have found it), against that which *ought to be* (in our own value system and/or that of the group we have studied). This recreates the original meaning of experimental in American culture. It is an examination of that which is manifest in man and his institutions in the light of expectations that go beyond measurement.

7. What Is Worthwhile?

After preaching twelve times a week for a year, John Leland was "sunken to great distress of mind." He wondered how to address a congregation of sinners in gospel style, and he felt that his preaching was not effectual. But when four school children and a young man made professions of faith during one of his services, he felt "both relief and courage."[1]

Without some way to assess our ceaseless activity, any professional person will feel distress of mind. At the Northeast Career Counseling Center, "How am I doing?" was the major question that clergy–clients raised with director Thomas Brown. At the Midwest Career Counseling Center, Frank Williams reported recurrent dissatisfaction from clergy because of limited opportunities for evaluation from others. They did not know if they were doing anything meaningful. Who thought they were producing a good program?[2]

What Do You Mean by a Good Program?

Elder Leland obtained relief and courage when he baptized five persons. That was the sure sign of success in 1806. We cannot count on the same agreement of criteria today. As Jeffrey Hadden found in the research for *Gathering Storm in the Churches*, laity and ministers of the same denomination disagree on desired goals for church and clergy. If we are going to rely on our evaluation, we must begin with some agreement on desired outcomes.

The desired outcomes will vary with our expectations of the program. Edgar W. Mills noted in an address on continuing education that his work as an evaluator included administrative, sponsor, and change goals. Any one of these would be appropriate for evaluation, but each should be distinguished in determining our answer to the question, "What is a good program?"

Administrative goals meet our expectations of the way in which a program is produced. Did people know what to expect and did they find it? Were the speakers well received? Was the program on schedule? How about the accommodations?

Many evaluations of special conferences and of Christian education in the local church will consist of these questions. They are significant as a measure of our implementation of intentions. They do not question the efficiency or the effectiveness of a program. That is, they do not measure benefits to the sponsor in terms of financial gain or good will (efficiency), nor do they tell us what people did as a result of this program (effectiveness).

Sponsor goals are more commonly stated in government and business as cost-effectiveness. If we put so much money into this community program, what will be the payoff? For example, will a federal grant of one hundred thousand dollars a year for a community mental health center result in a fifty-thousand-dollar decrease in long-term treatment of patients in a nearby state hospital and fifty thousand dollars in wages earned by citizens who would have been in the state hospital if they had not received supportive treatment in the mental health center so that they could keep their jobs?

Benefits to religious sponsors may or may not be measured financially. Some could be. An increase in gifts for the Episcopal Church in Canada seemed to be related to an attractive presentation of specific mission programs and a policy by which churches and individuals could designate gifts after a quota had been raised for general causes. Another anticipated example would be a jump in seminary revenue as ministers are attracted to doctor of ministry programs, far above the anticipated increase from recruitment for other graduate programs in theology.

Of course, one of the valued results of the doctoral program would go beyond finances to include increased support for seminary causes from established ministers who enrolled for this type of continuing education. There are a multitude of benefits to public relations built upon the gratitude of powerful graduates.

Sponsor benefits have many applications in a local congregation. Is the cost of a pastoral counseling program offset by increased giving from clients of the program to the sponsoring church? Did a recent legacy to the church come because of the goodwill built up by this program or for some other reason? During a stewardship campaign, is this program mentioned frequently by members as an example of what the church should be, or not?

Itinerant evangelists have been cost-effective for a long time. After so many meetings, an evangelist can predict the number of professions that will come from his meeting in churches of a certain size.

Any mention of revivals will bring a quick question: "But who was really changed as a result of that meeting?" When we begin to ask questions about observable changes in conduct or stability of membership after conversion, we are considering *change goals*. How has the attitude or action of a participant been modified as a direct result of this program? That's the tough and essential question of a change goal.

Where Do I Measure?

Change, sponsor, or administrative goals tell us what we are responsible for measuring. This is like the first general question in research, "Why did I undertake this study?" Then we ask, "What question am I trying to answer?" In an evaluation, this usually is answered by time—before, during, or after.[3]

Before a program begins, some measure of the congregation or survey of social conditions may be needed. This provides data for program planning and information which can be compared with later data to measure change. For example, a congregation may use the questions of Merton Strommen's Church Youth Research Center to determine what bothers youth the most, what they believe, what they think about the church and youth leaders.[4] This evaluation of youth could guide program planners in the congregation, increase the responsiveness of leaders to youth, and be a source of comparison with a later study of the same group or with the next group of young people who grow up in the church. Then we would know something about the changes in youth over a period of time or the difference between youth in the 1960s, 1970s, or 1980s.

Denominational self-study guides provide an evaluation of present conditions for the purpose of maintaining or increasing the congregation. We can predict the need for a new sanctuary or additional educational space from a survey of the ages of children in the community, the rate at which houses are being built, or utilities applied for. The survey will also pilot us toward changes in program for the aged, the divorced, or any group that is growing and perhaps neglected in the area.

This institutional information is not enough. Our

evaluation should also show the acceptance or resistance of the congregation to a sense of mission in the community, their sensitivity to social issues, the theological issues which are significant to them, and the areas of personal need in their lives. If we can obtain this dynamic data, we can plan *with* our people rather than *for* them. Changes can be presented on the basis of felt needs and personal commitment.

Richard Gorsuch and I developed a survey for local churches that considered attitudes toward society, traditional religion, the church program, and the intrinsic or extrinsic goal of personal faith. A congregation that used this as a guide for program development was both pleased and displeased. The leaders were encouraged to find many young adults who wanted the church to do something and who felt that religion was valuable for its own sake (intrinsic motivation). But it was disheartening to learn that persons who had been members of the church for a long time were more convinced that the church was confused.

At the time of the survey, the church was without a pastor. The leaders learned from the questionnaires that they could not identify any one direction in which the church should move when a pastor arrived. Instead, his first mission would be the establishment of some direction for the congregation. At the present time, few of the members had strong commitments to any program in church or community.[5]

But suppose we were already pastor of that church, and the leaders had agreed on the necessity of a new program. An evaluation during program growth would show us the relationship between stated goals and means of obtaining them. We might find, as the University of California Survey Research Center reported, that the formal goals are frequently subverted by the needs of a growing congregation to obtain institutional stability. The formal goal of community, the sense of closeness that was so desired by the suburbanites who started the church, seems to be lost when the large sanctuary is built and the organization is established.[6]

We could monitor this process as a pastor through progress reports on what happened, or by process notes on the ways that people talked to one another and responded to those in power. Sometimes the process is observed by members for research purposes or by students. When the results are reported, as in the Elmhurst Church controversy in Chicago, we can see what happens over a three-year period as a progressive pastor challenges—and loses—a complacent power structure in his congregation.[7]

In a process evaluation, we usually decide on the style of leadership that should be followed or the steps in program development that are desirable, and we record what happens. We may do this by ourselves or with a panel of judges who review our findings periodically and add their perspective. Or, as in the Elmhurst case discussed above, several participant observers may pool their observations.

Thomas Bennett requested periodic evaluations from pastors and lay members of leadership groups in a variety of churches. The purpose of meetings over the period of a year was to increase participation of the laity. The process notes showed a strong group when the minister talked about himself with his leadership and they supported him. But when he talked little of his concerns, and/or group leaders did not support him, the groups terminated in a few months.[8]

If you are beginning a doctor of ministry program on

new forms of ministry, you might look for colleagues who want to do the same thing, but with a different leadership style. You might have the *ideological style* that Grace Goodman found in her study of change in nine congregations.[9] That is, you are a strong leader with convictions of what is right. A study of program process in your church would probably show much resistance from lay leadership. Another student might prefer the *organizational style*. He would slowly adjust the system of his church. His field report would not be half completed by the time you had graduated—and were looking for another church. A charming person in your class might develop process notes about his *personalistic style*. His records should show some direct and dramatic changes in the lives of individuals which would be used as inspiration for institutional change.

There may be an important pastor in continuing education who would contribute the *political style* to this follow-up on Grace Goodman's categories. He would have the personal ability and enough leadership in his congregation to combine some of the three styles we have already described. Since this is complex, several observers would be needed to see what was going on as various leaders persuaded church factions to come along with a new program.

Process evaluation has also been used in denominational studies of Christian education. The Lutheran Longitudinal Study and others are surveyed and evaluated by Leonard Sibley and Allen Barton in chapters 21 and 22 of *Research on Religious Development*. Their excellent summaries, and others, make the encyclopedic book worth the price of purchase.

Will the results of all this study be worthwhile? Presbyterians and others tried to build evaluation into their new curriculum for the 1960s, but neither the developers nor the evaluators anticipated a drop in the sale of Christian education material. Some churches liked the study books so well that they kept them and reused them every few years. Result—no new sales. Other churches opted for the less demanding and more traditional Uniform Lesson Series which they obtained from independent publishing houses.

The massive reduction of denominational staff in the late sixties should increase our concern for outcome evaluation. What happens *after* our new program is in operation? Have people changed attitudes and/or actions, and in what direction?

The Ministry Studies Board developed outcome measures for five pioneer programs for clergy in community action. The impact of the programs was assessed in three steps. First, the staff identified a group of ministers who had similar characteristics to ministers in training. This would enable the staff to determine whether changes among the trainees could be attributed to the action program or to events outside the program. Second, the observable changes in the trainees and nontrainees were classified.

The change might be in personal characteristics. Did the minister have greater self-acceptance, grow in insight and in feeling for others? The empathy scales of Truax and Carkhuff are useful for this purpose.[10]

Other changes might be in ministerial role performance, in which the roles identified by Sam Blizzard are the criteria. The Ministry Study Board staff used a variety of performance measures, such as more effective use of community resources.[11]

Or the change might be in the social systems of which the minister is a part. What development has occurred in lay leadership? Are they more sympathetic and involved in community projects?

The third step in outcome assessment was a comparison of changes among ministers in training and the comparable group of clergy not in training.

Can I Continue?

After we know what we are responsible for, and have decided on the timing of our evaluation (before, during, or after), we must consider three issues that maintain evaluation as a form of research and keep us moving beyond the usual stagnation of routine record-keeping.

(1) A *control* group is very significant for the type of evaluation that is labeled outcome research. How effective is a particular program? Gus Verdery raised this question about clinical pastoral education that extends over six months or a year with sessions for training held less often than in the full-time, concentrated sessions that have been traditional for three months.[12] The evaluation of extended training should include measures of the more concentrated training and measures of ministers who are not in training. Without this latter control group, we would not know if changes occurred because of church experience and personal maturity, or because a minister was in training—or some of both.

Psychotherapy research has generated some lively debates through the use of control groups, or the comparison of professional and nonprofessional. One controversy has arisen over the evidence that the nonprofessional volunteer, a college student or housewife, is more effective in the rehabilitation of chronic mental patients than the professional staff.[13]

An example of control groups in the training of clergymen as counselors is reported in *Innovations* (Fall,

1975). Dr. Merton Strommen divided counselors by the amount of training they received for their work with adolescents. The degree of change for youth was as great in counseling provided by clergymen who had received the full range of training and those who had received training in a program that was only half as long.

Another dispute centers around the effectiveness of *any* psychotherapy. H. J. Eysenck, a British psychologist, had hypothesized that all the so-called therapeutic effects of psychotherapy could be explained by a natural restorative process which takes place with or without psychotherapy. In 1975, two researchers sought to test his theory by comparing the improvement of patients who completed a course of therapy with patients who were seen one time and never returned for treatment. Although the improvement of patients in therapy was significant, the improvement of persons who dropped out after one interview was almost as great when they were seen several years later.[14]

(2) The *criterion* question can often be resolved if we search the literature for related studies that have developed operational definitions. For example, Roy Whitman and Linda Viney showed that attitude change is not very significant in measuring the success of community mental health workshops. The professionals who attend such meetings are already persuaded that community work is a good thing. The change is not in attitude, but in practice and function. When the research team questioned students several months after the workshop, changes were observed in development of after-care services, more discussion with colleagues about community mental health, more presentations of mental health ideas in staff meetings, more contacts in the community with other helping professions, a reduction of waiting lists, more cooperation with other agencies.[15]

Some "doing" measures would reduce the subjectivity of some religious evaluations that state, "Student will integrate ego and superego functions and be in touch with his feelings." The operational definition of this blurb may be the student's lack of guilt when he snarls at his supervisor and uses four-letter words to portray his hostility. More objective criteria were developed by Chester Raber when he measured the effectiveness of an introductory course in pastoral care. His purpose was to find evidence that students could identify problems presented to them by patients or parishioners, as described in their comments on verbatim interviews that were given to Mr. Raber by the students. Also, the students should be able to respond in a way that showed their patient or parishioner that they understood the problem or feeling that was presented. Finally, the students should be able to offer some interpretation of what they heard or give some information that would be acceptable to the client. Mr. Raber and three associates read two interviews of each student, one presented to him on the day that he entered the class and the other on the day of his final examination. The student wrote comments on the interviews or presented his own answers to some of the comments by a patient or parishioner.

In a church or institution, a pastor may draw up a list of activities or desired outcomes of his ministry, either alone or with church members or institutional staff. When such a list was developed in one general hospital, the chaplains gave more emphasis to their psychological counseling than did the staff and patients, who emphasized the traditional activities of prayer, routine visitation, ministry to the dying, and chapel services.[16]

(3) The third condition for a completed evaluation is *conscientiousness* in reporting events. When one promi-

nent pastor finished his doctoral program, he said, "I wish I could talk to every professor and student in this program and tell them to start writing down everything related to their field project from the day they begin to think about it. I was so accustomed to getting things going, and then evaluating it, that I lost the first six months of my work, which would have been the most valuable, because then we were deciding what we were going to do and why. It's tough—and unreliable—to reconstruct all that from memory."

Who Will Help Me?

The plaintive remark of this pastor is a challenge for more continuing emphasis upon evaluation in our everyday ministry. There are times when we conduct special studies on a new program or survey a church field before a new pastor arrives. But where is the regular expectation that we can set forth our work in a way that pastor and people can decide strength and weakness?

The strongest support for routine evaluation can come from denominational organizations at the local, regional, and national level. The continuity and status of a minister's professional life is centered in the denomination. That which he reports is a sign of what his peers and superiors approve. If his reports are an accurate reflection of the dynamic concerns of his congregation, his community, and his own professional life, then he will have a regular answer to the question, "How am I doing?"

Routine church records and report forms can provide this support, but do they? In a report to the Statisticians of American Religious Bodies in 1967, I found the forty-seven annual report forms of Protestant, Roman Catholic, and Jewish religious bodies to favor membership statistics and money pledged. This was true even of denominations that were most active in the "church in mission" movement. United Church of Christ forms, for example, had no questions on community involvement or ecumenical endeavor. On the other hand, the American Baptists and Southern Presbyterians asked about involvement of the church in social action.

The single most important institutional question was, "How's your Sunday school growing?" The question was asked in a dozen ways, with special categories for age groups. Only one denomination, the Church of the Brethren, asked, "What's going on because these groups are meeting?"

Individual religious experience and pastoral care had no place in denominational forms of the 1960s. The reports made it clear that the denominations were evaluating the pastors, the churches, and themselves by the depersonalized, social success standards of an expanding economy. But it is now possible to record more dynamic data; to ask questions about the relations of Christians to one another in the church, to other faith groups, to people in need in the community; or to record the spiritual development of individuals.

The expectations of experimental religion can become part of the routine reporting and occasional studies in depth that will evaluate the church and its ministry for pastor, people, denomination, and any interested inquirer after the place of religion in life.

Postscript: What Shall I Write?

When an English traveler asked a Turkish cadi for statistical information, the Oriental official gave an answer that we should read before the preparation of any manuscript or the presentation of research findings to any audience:

"My Illustrious Friend, and Joy of my Liver!

"The thing you ask of me is both difficult and useless. Although I have passed all my days in this place I neither counted the houses nor inquired into the number of the inhabitants; and as to what one person loads on his mules and the other stows away in the bottom of his ship, that is no business of mine. But, above all, as to the previous history of this city, God only knows the amount of dirt and confusion that the infidels may have eaten before the coming of the sword of Islam. It were unprofitable for us to inquire into it. . . .

"But thou wilt say unto me, Stand aside, O man, for I am more learned than thou art, and have seen more things. If thou thinkest that thou art in this respect better than I am, thou art welcome. I praise God and I seek not that which I require not. Thou art learned in the things I care not for; and for that which thou hast seen, I spit upon it. Will much knowledge create thee a double belly or wilt thou seek Paradise with thine eyes? Oh my friend! if thou wilt be happy, say, There is no God but God! Do no evil, and thus wilt thou fear neither man nor death, for surely thine hour will come." [1]

Write your report for people who think as this Turkish cadi. Ask yourself these questions:

(1) Did I learn anything from this study?_____ (yes) _____ (no)

(2) If the answer is no, read no further.

(3) If the answer is yes, put down on one page the significance of your search.

(4) Would anyone else learn from reading this one page? _____ (yes) _____ (no)

(5) If the answer is no, enjoy your treasure in secret.

(6) If the answer is yes, state in one paragraph why he would learn something from your study.

(7) Combine questions 3 and 6 into an abstract of your report which could be submitted for publication and will also be placed first in the full report of your findings.

Add this much to the abstract or introduction:

(8) Who were the subjects of the research?

(9) What operations were carried out in reference to them?

(10) What results ensued?

When you have done this, the general audience for your study will be satisfied. But those who have interests beyond that of the Turkish cadi will want to know more. Tell them where to obtain a copy of the full report which should include answers to the following questions:[2]

(1) What pertinent research preceded this study, and how will your work be distinctive?

(2) Describe your research procedures in a way that another person could follow you exactly. This will include statements about objectives, sample, design, data collection, and method of analysis.

(3) Include your questionnaire or an exact statement of the questions you asked and the way in which you asked them. If you used a standardized test, tell where it may be obtained or where it is described.

(4) Just what did you find? Include negative as well as positive findings. Suggestions on the way to portray

statistical results may be found in Hans Zeisel, *Say It With Figures* (New York: Harper & Row, 1957).

(5) What is the relationship between what you found and the studies of others? Seek help from a knowledgeable person in this field of study. You probably will know such a person from following the procedures recommended earlier in chapter 4, section 2, "What Are You Looking For?"

(6) Tell what you are going to do on the basis of what you have found and what others might do. Keep that part of the study always before you as a guide to experimental religion in your own life.

Your writing will have demonstrated one part of professional wisdom, "No action without investigation." Now complete it, "No inquiry without action."

Notes

Chapter 1

[1] Jonathan Edwards, *Religious Affections* (New Haven: Yale University Press, 1959), p. 452.

[2] James E. Dittes, "Psychology of Religion," *The Handbook of Social Psychology*, ed. Gardner Lindzey and E. Aronson, 5 vols. (Reading, Mass.: Addison-Wesley Publishing Co., 1969), V, 620.

[3] Edwards, *Religious Affections*, p. 453.

[4] Perry Miller, *Jonathan Edwards* (Westport, Conn.: Greenwood Press, 1973), p. 177.

[5] Pauline Young, *Scientific Social Surveys and Research*, 2nd ed. rev. (Englewood Cliffs, N.J.: Prentice-Hall, 1949), pp. 203-4.

[6] *Ibid.*, p. 16.

[7] See, for example, Thomas Luckmann, *The Invisible Religion* (New York: Macmillan Co., 1967); John J. Sullivan, "Two Psychologies and the Study of Religion," *Journal for the Scientific Study of Religion*, 1 (1961).

[8] David Bakan, *On Method* (San Francisco: Jossey-Bass, 1967), pp. xiii, 28, 85, 158; a brief summary of the use of empiricism in religion is Jack P. Hanford, "A Synoptic Approach; Resolving Problems in Empirical and Phenomenological Approaches to the Psychology of Religion," *Journal for the Scientific Study of Religion*, 14 (1975): 219-27.

[9] Joseph Haroutunian, "Theology and the American Experience," *Criterion* (Winter 1964).

[10] Thomas Campbell and Yoshio Fukuyama, *The Fragmented Layman* (Philadelphia: Pilgrim Press, 1970), p. 197. Additional examples of questionnaire and interview schedules may be found in tests listed under the names of Allport, Rokeach, etc., in Oscar K. Buros, *Tests in Print* (Highland Park, N.J.: Grython Press, 1974). Discussions of their interpretation may be found in Milton Rokeach, *The Nature of Values* (New York: Free Press, 1973); "Value Systems in Religion," *Review of Religious Research* (Fall 1969); "A Theory of Organization and Change Within Value-Attitude Systems," *The Journal of Social Issues* (January 1968); Richard A. Hunt, "The Interpretation of the Religious Scale of the Allport-Vernon-Lindzey Study of Values," *Journal for the Scientific Study of Religion*, 7 (1968); Russell O. Allen and Bernard Spilka, "Committed and Consensual Religion," *Ibid.*, 6 (1967). For a review on measurement of moral values see Stephen M. Tittle and Gerald A.

Mendelsohn, "Measurement of Moral Values: A Review and Critique," *Psychological Bulletin* (July 1966): 22-35.

[11] Samuel Mueller, "Relevance, Community Organization and Sociology," *Christian Century*, (October 11, 1967): 1282.

[12] According to Warner Heston's study of forty-six young pastors, cited in Mark Rouch, *Competent Ministry* (Nashville: Abingdon, 1974), p. 111.

[13] The Episcopal Church, Strategic Research Services Group, "The Top Priority Empirical Research Project on Clergy" (Darien, Connecticut: 1970), p. 3.

[14] This is the affirmation of the Director of Doctor of Ministry Programs, United Theological Seminary of the Twin Cities, Clyde Steckel.

[15] Carl Rogers, "Reinhold Niebuhr's The Self and the Dramas of History," *Pastoral Psychology* (June 1958): 15.

[16] *Ibid.*, p. 24.

[17] *Ibid.*, p. 25-26.

[18] David Ernsberger, "Evaluation in the Church," *Austin Seminary Bulletin* (September 1974): 5.

[19] *Theological Education* (Summer 1974): 284-85.

Chapter 2

[1] See James E. Dittes, "A Symposium on Pastoral Research," *Journal of Pastoral Care* (December 1973): 255 ff. For a discussion of appropriate measures, see Young, *Scientific Social Surveys*, pp. 375-77.

[2] Dittes, *Journal of Pastoral Care*, p. 254; Robert Bermudes, "A Ministry to the Repeatedly Grief-Stricken," *Ibid.*, pp. 218-28.

[3] Samuel Southard, "Religious Concern in the Psychoses," *Journal of Pastoral Care*, 10 (Winter 1956): 228 ff.

[4] The construction of an index of devotional orientation is described in Campbell and Fukuyama, *Fragmented Layman*, p. 70.

[5] For an example of factor and cluster analysis, see Morton King, "Measuring the Religious Variable," *Journal for the Scientific Study of Religion*, 6 (1967): 178-85. The procedures of electronic data processing are described by Earl Babbie in chapter 10 of *Survey Research Methods* (Belmont, Cal.: Wadworth Publishing Co., 1973).

[6] The construction of such indexes are detailed by Babbie, *Research Methods*, chap. 14.

[7] The six requirements discussed in the preceding pages are adapted from Bernard Berelson and Gary Steinor, *Human Behavior: An Investigation of Scientific Findings* (New York: Harcourt Brace and World, 1964), pp. 16-18.

Chapter 3

[1] William James, *The Varieties of Religious Experience*, 1902. The challenge to creative empiricism in religion was also presented by Henry

Nelson Wieman in *Religious Inquiry: Some Explorations* (Boston: Beacon Press, 1968).

[2]See Samuel Southard, "Personal Life of the Frontier Ministry," *Journal for the Scientific Study of Religion*, 10 (1966): 213-23.

[3]Liston Mills, "The Relationship of Discipline to Pastoral Care in Frontier Churches, 1800-1850: A Preliminary Study," *Pastoral Psychology*, 16 (December 1965): 22-34.

[4]A pastor in the county later explained that people who moved away to the cities would keep their names on the church rolls so that they would be eligible for burial in the rural church cemeteries that dotted the countryside.

[5]A pioneering text is Bernard Berelson, *Content Analysis in Communications Research* (New York: The Free Press, 1952).

[6]A summary of the Hadden survey is "A Protestant Paradox—Divided They Merge," *Trans-Action*, 5 (July/August 1967): 63-69.

[7]Samuel Z. Klausner found that the self-administered questionnaire is the most popular tool for the study of religion. See "Methods of Data Collection in Studies of Religion," *Journal for the Scientific Study of Religion*, 7 (1964).

[8]See Robert Abelson, "Computers, Polls and Public Opinion—Some Puzzles and Paradoxes," *Trans-Action* (September 1968).

[9]For more on behavior measure vs. questionnaire, see Lindzey and Aronson, *Handbook of Social Psychology*, II, 54 ff.

[10]Edwards could be a model for H. Richard Niebuhr's *The Responsible Self* (New York: Harper & Row, 1963).

[11]See Perry Miller, "The Rhetoric of Sensation," *Errand into the Wilderness* (New York: Harper & Brothers, 1956).

[12]Anton Boisen, *Religion in Crisis and Custom* (New York: Harper & Row, 1963), p. 21. A plea for more studies in the tradition of Boisen is made by Wayne Oates and Andrew Lester, *Pastoral Care in Crucial Human Situations* (Valley Forge, Pa.: Judson Press, 1969).

[13]John Niles Bartholomew, "A Study of Planning Techniques for Local Congregations," mimeographed (New York: Institute of Strategic Studies, Board of National Missions, United Presbyterian Church, 1967). For a review of the contribution of Paul Douglass, see Edmund deS. Brunner, "Harland Paul Douglass: Pioneer Researcher in the Sociology of Religion," *Review of Religious Research*, 1 (1959).

[14]Donald Metz, *New Congregations: Security and Mission in Conflict* (Philadelphia: Westminster Press, 1967).

[15]See Thomas Wieser, *Planning for Mission* (New York: U.S. Conference for the World Council of Churches, 1966), pp. 205-14.

[16]See the manual by Gerald Jud for the United Churches of Christ, "The Local Church and God's Mission," and his general guide for planning, *Pilgrim's Process* (Philadelphia: United Church Press, 1967). In conversational style with many practical examples, Lyle Schaller

offers guidance on *Parish Planning* (Nashville: Abingdon, 1971), decision-making, *The Decision-Makers* (Nashville: Abingdon, 1974), and change in church and community, *The Change Agent* (Nashville: Abingdon, 1972).

[17]Bartholomew, "Study of Planning Techniques," p. 27.

[18]Grace Goodman, *Rocking the Ark* (New York: Division of Evangelism, Board of National Missions, United Presbyterian Church, 1968), p. 200.

[19]Bonnie Strickland and S. Shaffer, *Journal for the Scientific Study of Religion*, 10 (1971): 366-69.

[20]Bruno Heidik, "Religious Orientation and Mental Illness: A Comparison of Three Selected Groups" (M.A. thesis, University of Maryland, 1974). Heidik was not satisfied with the instrument as a means of discriminating between intrinsic and extrinsic religion. For a discussion of intrinsic-extrinsic, see *Journal for the Scientific Study of Religion*, 10 (1971).

Chapter 4

[1]Anton Boisen, *Problems in Religion and Life* (Nashville & New York: Abingdon-Cokesbury Press, 1946), p. 37.

[2]Samuel Southard, "A Pastor's First Year of Counseling," *Religion in Life*, 26 (1956): 553.

[3]*Ibid.*

[4]Chaplain Tisdale found eight entries that met the criteria (personal correspondence, April 3, 1975).

[5]See Gibson Winter, "Methodological Reflections on the Religious Factor," *Journal for the Scientific Study of Religion*, 1 (1962); Morton B. King and Richard Hunt, *Measuring Religious Dimensions* (Dallas: Southern Methodist University, 1972). The process by which a test instrument is refined can be seen in Morton King, "Measuring the Religious Variable: Amended Findings," *Journal for the Scientific Study of Religion*, 8 (1969): 321-23; Hunt and King, "Measuring the Religious Variable: Replication," *Ibid.*, 11 (1972): 240-51; Hunt and King, "Measuring the Religious Variable: National Replication," *Ibid.*, 14 (1975): 13-22. A particular issue for sociologists of religion has been the dimensions or religiosity as presented by Glock and Stark. Their typology of multidimensional religiosity is challenged by Richard Clayton and James Gladden in a 1974 article of the *Journal for the Scientific Study of Religion*, pp. 135-43.

Chapter 5

[1]The elements necessary in medical studies are briefly described by Richard Rada and Vernon Jones, *Hospital and Community Psychiatry* (May 1975): 305-6.

[2]Clarence Drummond, "Developing a Model of Church Ministry in a

Racially Transitional Community" (D. Min. field project, Southern Baptist Theological Seminary, 1974), and personal interview, February 20, 1975.

[3]*Ibid.,* p. 93.

[4] An entertaining and instructive guide to sampling and sampling statistics is Morris James Slonim, *Sampling* (New York: Simon & Schuster, 1960).

[5] Hugh Burns, "A Factor Analytic Study of Religious Attitudes Among Psychiatric Patients and Normals," *Journal for the Scientific Study of Religion,* 8 (1969): 165.

[6] See Dittes, "Psychology of Religion," *Handbook of Social Psychology,* V, 602-59.

[7] Victor B. Kline and James M. Richards, Jr., "A Factor-Analytic Study of Religious Belief and Behavior," *Journal of Personality and Social Psychology,* 1: 569-78.

[8] Russell Allen and Bernard Spilka, "Committed and Consensual Religion," *Journal for the Scientific Study of Religion,* 6 (1967): 199-200.

[9] Some suggestions for unobtrusive research are given by Hubert Blalock, Jr., in chapter 2 of *An Introduction to Social Research* (Englewood Cliffs, N.J.: Prentice-Hall, 1970).

Chapter 6

[1] Jackson Carroll and Gerald Jenkins, "The Development of Religious Commitment: Some Exploratory Research," *Journal of Pastoral Care* (December 1973): 236-52.

[2] An example of variability between populations is presented by John Gleason in "Religious Inventory Research Project—Progress Report," *Association of Mental Health Chaplains Newsletter* (Spring, 1971): 61-62.

[3] For more discussion of correlation, see Blalock, *Social Research,* chap. 5; Leon Festinger and Daniel Katz, *Research Methods in the Behavioral Sciences* (New York: Holt, Rinehart and Winston, 1953), pp. 424-66.

[4] Slonim, *Sampling,* p. 30. For an example of the way in which correlations are often the result of the researcher's assumptions, see James Dittes, review of *Christian Beliefs and Anti-Semiticism* by Charles Glock, *Review of Religious Research* (1967): 183-87.

[5] Robert Mitchell, "Age and the Ministry," *Review of Religious Research* (Spring 1967): 168.

[6] Roy Whitman and Linda Viney, "The Teaching of Doers," *Archives of General Psychiatry,* 24 (April 1971): 379-84.

[7] *Explorations in Ministry* (San Francisco: Chandler Publishing Co., 1964), pp. 53-55.

[8] See Abraham Kaplan's discussion of explanation, in *Conduct of Inquiry,* pp. 345-69.

[9]Joachim Wach, *Types of Religious Experience: Christian and Non-Christian* (Chicago: University of Chicago Press, 1951), pp. 48-57. An extensive collection of excerpts from scholarly writings on religion may be found in the two-volume collection of Jacques Waardenburg, *Classical Approaches to the Study of Religion: Aims, Methods, and Theories of Research* (The Hague: Mouton, 1973 and 1974).

[10]Gibson Winter, "Methodological Reflection on 'The Religious Factor,'" *Journal for the Scientific Study of Religion*, 1 (1962): 60-61. Winter is challenged by J. Paul Williams in the Spring 1963 issue of the same journal.

Chapter 7

[1]L. F. Green, ed., *The Writings of the Late Elder John Leland* (New York: G. W. Wood, 1845), p. 33.

[2]Donald P. Smith, *Clergy in the Cross Fire* (Philadelphia: The Westminster Press, 1973) p. 144.

[3] See David Ernsberger, "Evaluation in the Church, "*Austin Seminary Bulletin*, faculty edition (September 1974): 5-31.

[4]The Church Youth Research Center types out an analysis of each score, compares composite scores between churches, and provides interpretations of scores for a nominal charge. Write to 122 West Franklin Street; Minneapolis, Minnesota 55404.

[5]A comprehensive study of attitudes among Lutherans is reported by Merton Strommen in *A Study of Generations*. A questionnaire on change in the church, which includes the value survey of Milton Rokeach, has been prepared by E. W. Hutchinson, Bureau of Community Research, Pacific School of Religion.

[6]Donald L. Metz, "Goal Subversion in New Church Development" (Berkeley, Cal.: Research Center Monograph M-11, 1965), p. 95.

[7]*Chicago Theological Seminary Register* (June 1966).

[8]"Project Laity," National Council of Churches, 1961.

[9]Goodman, *Rocking the Ark,* pp. 211-14.

[10]For example, see Roman M. Paur, "A Pre-Post Assessment of the Effects of Short Term Training Experiences on Indices of Personality and Counseling Behavior in Nonprofessional Trainees," as reported in John Florell, *Pastoral Care and Counseling Abstracts* (Richmond, Va.: Virginia Institute of Pastoral Care, 1973).

[11]J. Alan Winter, "Clergy in Action Training" (New York: IDOC, 1971), pp.61ff.

[12]Minutes of the Southeast Region ACPE Research Committee (April 12, 1975).

[13]A review of the evidence is provided by Averil Karisruher, "The Nonprofessional as a Psychotherapeutic Agent," *American Journal of Community Psychology*, 2 (1974). Also see the studies of Ernest G. Poser, "The Effect of Therapists' Training on Group Therapeutic Outcome,"

Journal of Consulting Psychology, 30 (1966); Jerome M. Siegel, "Mental Health Volunteers as Change Agents," *American Journal of Community Psychology*, 1 (1973); Robert Carkhuff and Charles Truax, "Lay Mental Health Counseling," *Journal of Consulting Psychology*, 29 (1965).

[14]David H. Malan et. al., "Psychodynamic Changes in Untreated Neurotic Patients," *Archives of General Psychiatry*, 32 (January 1975): 110ff.

[15]Ray Whitman and Linda Viney, "The Teaching of Doers," *Archives of General Psychiatry*, 24 (April 1971): 382.

[16]Raymond G. Carey, "Hospital Chaplains: Who Needs Them?" (Park Ridge, Ill.: Department of Pastoral Care, Lutheran General Hospital, 1972), pp. 27-28.

Postscript

[1]Richard Cabot, *Honesty* (New York: The Macmillian Co., 1938), pp. 116-17.

[2]For example, studies in the field of pastoral care may be reported through the Research Index Catalog, available in seminaries and center of clinical pastoral education. Forms for the report of information on research studies are available from the Virginia Institute of Pastoral Care; 507 North Lombardy Street; Richmond, Virginia 23220.

Some Suggested Readings

Theory and General Surveys

Babbie, Earl. *Survey Research Methods.* Belmont, Cal.: Wadsworth Publishing Co., 1973.

A general text with specific references to questionnaire design and data processing. Both this volume and Babbie's *Practice of Social Research* (1974) contain overviews of statistical methods in the final chapters. Many research terms are defined in the glossary of *Research Methods.*

Barzun, Jacques, and Graff, Henry. *The Modern Researcher.* New York: Harcourt Brace Jovanovich, 1957.

Since many graduate papers require some historical survey of a question, Barzun and Graff provide help in historical search, organization, and reporting.

Butterfield, Herbert. *The Origins of Modern Science.* New York: The Macmillan Co., 1960.

This book illustrates central issues in the formation and definition of scientific inquiry.

Kaplan, Abraham. *The Conduct of Inquiry.* San Francisco: Chandler, 1964.

This volume is more philosophical than Butterfield's *Origins.*

Paradis, Adrian A. *The Research Handbook.* New York: Funk & Wagnalls, 1966.

Guides the beginning student through reference sources of the community: library, documents, maps, reports.

Young, Pauline. *Scientific Social Surveys and Research: An*

Introduction to the Background, Content, Methods, Principles and Analysis of Social Studies. 4th rev. ed. Englewood Cliffs, N.J.: Prentice-Hall, 1966.

Provides an overview of many methods of social research.

Research Design

Blalock, Hubert. *Introduction to Social Research.* Englewood Cliffs, N.J.: Prentice-Hall, 1970.

Principles of experimental design and advances in research from computer technology are presented in Blalock's *Introduction.*

Miller, Delbert. *Handbook of Research Design and Social Measurement.* New York: David McKay Co., 1970.

Miller's *Handbook* reviews numerous issues and also provides information on foundations, journals, and professional associations.

Selye, Hans. *The Stress of Life.* New York: McGraw-Hill Book Co., 1956.

This practical volume presents the assumptions, experimental methods, and practical applications that Selye related to one medical syndrome—stress.

Shontz, Franklin. *Research Methods in Personality.* New York: Appleton-Century-Crofts, 1965.

Stouffer, Samuel. *Social Research to Test Ideas.* New York: The Free Press, 1962.

The process of ingenuity unfolds as you read this book.

Questionnaires

Gallup, George. *What My People Think: A Gallup Survey Manual.* Princeton, N.J.: American Institute of Public Opinion, 1971.

A summary of survey research methods for clergy.

Oppenheim, A. N. *Questionnaire Design and Attitude Measurement.* New York: Basic Books, 1966.

Treats this popular methodology of ministers, psychologists, and sociologists.

Payne, Stanley. *The Art of Asking Questions.* Princeton, N.J.: Princeton University Press, 1951.

Silverman, William. "Catalog."

A catalog of research instruments used in survey or questionnaire studies of religion has been assembled by William Silverman, Department of Sociology at Kean College in Union, New Jersey 07083.

Union College Character Research Project.

The Union College Character Research Project (207 State Street; Schenectady, New York 12305) offers packaged research projects; these include statements of purpose, instructions for administration, questionnaires, and methods of scoring and interpretation. Some of the packets currently available are: "Curriculum Revision Through Research," "Basic Tools for Creative Research," "Data Analysis," "On Determining Where You Are Going" (evaluation), "Barber Scales of Self-Regard for Preschool Children."

Participant Observation

Boisen, Anton. *Problems in Religion and Life.* Nashville & New York: Abingdon-Cokesbury Press, 1946.

Boisen details the questions that should be in the mind of any community observer.

Lofland, John. *Analyzing Social Settings.* Belmont, Cal.: Wadsworth Publishing Co., 1971.

McCall, George, and Simmons, J. L., ed. *Issues in Participant Observation: A Text and Reader.* Reading, Mass.: Addison-Wesley, 1969.

Includes selections of field research projects.

Webb, Eugene, et al. *Unobtrusive Measures.* Chicago: Rand McNally & Co., 1966.

Describes participant observation and content analysis.

119

Interviewing

Hyman, Herman. *Interviewing in Social Research.* Chicago: University of Chicago Press, 1967.

Investigates some of the problems in this difficult area.

Content Analysis

Stollak, Gary, et al., ed. *Psychotherapy Research.* Chicago: Rand McNally & Co., 1966.

Selected readings discuss content analysis and process research.

Analysis of Interviews, Therapy, Group Process

Bales, Robert. *Interaction Process Analysis: A Method for the Study of Small Groups.* Reading, Mass.: Addison-Wesley, 1950.

Berelson, Bernard. *Content Analysis in Communications Research.* New York: The Free Press, 1952.

A classic.

Rogers, Carl. *On Becoming a Person.* Boston: Houghton Mifflin, 1961.

Carl Rogers has been a pioneer in this area. See especially part 5 of this book.

Statistics

In addition to the recommended texts at the conclusion of chapter 5, see:

Anderson, James. *Research Design and Analysis in the Behavioral Sciences.* University Park, N.M.: New Mexico State University, July 1967.

An annotated bibliography on *Research Design* by James Anderson is available from the Research Center at New Mexico State University. The contents will lead ministers to technical articles on measurement, design, and analysis.

Andrews, Frank M., et al. *A Guide for Selecting Statistical Techniques for Analyzing Social Science Data.* Ann Arbor, Mich.: Institute of Social Research, 1975.

The search for an appropriate statistical technique is aided through the "decision tree" which consists of sixteen pages of sequential questions and answers which lead the user to an appropriate strategy.

Pelletier, Paula, and Rattenbury, Judith. *Data Processing in the Social Sciences.* Ann Arbor, Mich.: Institute of Social Research, 1974.

If you want to know how to use a computer, this guide assumes no previous knowledge on your part.

Zeisel, Hans. *Say It with Figures.* New York: Harper & Row, 1957.

Evaluation and Planning

Jud, Gerald. *Pilgrim's Process.* Philadelphia: United Church Press, 1967.

Schaller, Lyle. *Parish Planning.* Nashville: Abingdon, 1971.

Weiss, Carroll. *Evaluation Research.* Englewood Cliffs, N.J.: Prentice-Hall, 1972.

Wieser, Thomas. *Planning for Mission.* New York: World Council of Churches, 1966.

Survey of Religious Research

Strommen, Merton, ed. *Research on Religious Development.* New York: Hawthorn Books, 1971.

The most comprehensive volume available.

Index